I0243553

John O'Neill

A First Japanese Book for English Students

John O'Neill

A First Japanese Book for English Students

ISBN/EAN: 9783337163600

Printed in Europe, USA, Canada, Australia, Japan

Cover: Foto ©ninafisch / pixelio.de

More available books at **www.hansebooks.com**

A First Japanese Book

For English Students.

By John O'Neill.

A First Japanese Book

for English Students;

CONSISTING OF

(1) The *Text* of a *Buddhist Sermon* in the colloquial dialect, printed in *Japan*, in cursive *Chinese* & *hiragana* characters;
(2) An interleaved *Transcription* in *English* letters;
(3) A *Literal Translation*, with
(4) Interlinear *Glosses*,
(5) Explanatory *Notes*, &
(6) A Copious *Vocabulary*—

BY

John O'Neill.

WITH

(7) Tables of the *Japanese hiragana* & *katakana* characters.

LONDON:
published by *Harrison & Sons*, at
No. 59, Pall Mall.

1874.

INTRODUCTION.

§ 1. This is a book written by a student for students, and if it can lay claim to any of the advantages, it must also confess to the drawbacks inseparable from such a production. On the one hand, there are no pretensions to advanced scholarship, but, on the other, minute care has been taken to elucidate the numerous difficulties that seem insuperable to a beginner, but are almost forgotten by the time mastery is acquired. Whatever be the merits and demerits of the publication, it is believed that the idea worked out is now for the first time applied to Japanese.

§ 2. The book consists of a Japanese text cut on wood and printed in Japan, interleaved by a transcription in English letters, and accompanied by a literal translation, with interlinear glosses, running, clause by clause, sentence by sentence, and line by line, with the Japanese; explanatory notes at the foot of each page, and a full vocabulary of nearly a thousand words. By the kindness of Mr. W. G. Aston, the Interpreter to our Legation in Japan,* I am enabled to add tables of the hiragana and katakana characters from his Grammar of the Japanese Written Language (London, 1872).

§ 3. The Japanese text is one of Kiu-Ō's *Dō-Wa*, or Path Discourses (*michi no hanashi*), sermons on the Path of Morality,—an expression analogous to our "path of virtue" and "narrow way,"—by the preacher Kiu-Ō, a priest belonging to the Shingakŭ sect, which professes to combine all that is excellent in the Buddhist, Confucian, and Shintō teaching. This sect maintains the original excellence of the human heart,—a doctrine the reverse of that of original sin,—and teaches that we should endeavour to revert to our original state, and that we have only to follow the dictates of the conscience (*hon-shin*) implanted in us at birth,† in order to follow the right path.

* Without whose kind encouragement, advice, and assistance, this book would perhaps never have seen the light.

† Ichido hon-shin wo go yetokŭ nasaremasuru to, kimĭyōna mono ja. Sermon, p 19. Hito tabi hon-shin wo yetokŭ sureba, naranŭ koto wa naranŭ to shiri, nangina koto wa nangi to gaten suru. Ibid, p. 32. See also pp. 21, 22, *et passim*.

§ 4. A Sermon has been chosen as the groundwork of this First Japanese Book, because sermons such as the Kiu-Ō Dō-Wa and the Shingakū Dō-Wa are some of the best and most easily accessible of the few books which are published in the colloquial dialect, and because it is to this dialect, the grammar of which differs much from that of the written language, that the practical student should first address himself. The Kiu-Ō Dō-wa are written in the spoken language of the Central Provinces.

§ 5. The Sermon has long been a popular institution in Japan. Occasionally delivered as part of a service on special days of the month, sermons are more frequently preached in courses, the delivery occupying about a fortnight, during which two sermons are given every day. Frequently the preachers are itinerant priests who go about the towns and villages, lecturing in the main hall of some temple or in the guest-room of the resident priest. Mitford, in his *Tales of Old Japan*, gives the following account of a sermon, preached in the Chō-ō-ji temple at Yedo by a priest of the Buddhist sect of Nichiren :—

> In one corner was a low writing desk at which sat, or rather squatted, a lay clerk. . .
>
> The congregation seemed poor enough. It was principally composed of old women, nuns with bald shiny pates and grotesque faces, a few petty tradesmen, and half a dozen chubby children, perfect little models of decorum and devoutness.
>
> Fire-boxes and spittoons* were freely handed about, so that half an hour which passed before the sermon began, was agreeably spent. . . . .
>
> The lay clerk sat himself down by the hanging drum and to its accompaniment began intoning the prayer "Na Mu Miyô Hô Ren Go Kiyô," the congregation fervently joining in unison with him. These words, repeated over and over again, are the distinctive prayer of the Buddhist sect of Nichiren, to which the temple Chô-ô-ji is dedicated. They are approximations to Sanscrit sounds†, and have no meaning in Japanese, nor do the worshippers in using them know their precise value.
>
> Soon the preacher, gorgeous in red and white robes, made his appearance, following an acolyte who carried the sacred book, called *Hokkê* (upon which the sect of Nichiren is founded), on a tray covered with scarlet and gold brocade. Having bowed to the sacred picture which hung over the *tokonoma*—that portion of the Japanese room which is raised

* The preacher terminates the first of the Shingakū Sermons by saying, Tōseba nagō narimasū yuye, madzu ippuku itashimashō : As it will be long if we go through with it, let us first smoke a pipe. I. O'N.

† By the kind help of Professor Cowell and a learned Japanese, I am enabled to offer an explanation of the prayer, *Namu mīyo hō Ren-ge kīyō*. *Namu* is for namaḥ, the ordinary Sanskrit word at the beginning of ascriptions of praise, and means 'Hail!' or 'Glory!'; *mīyo*, 'efficient,' is a translation of sad, 'good,' 'true,' 'real' or 'existent'; *hō*, 'means,' *i.e.*, means of obtaining purification and nirváṇa, translates dharma, 'law'; *Ren-ge* is puṇḍaríka, 'lotus'; *kīyō*, 'book,' is sútra. The prayer is thus, Namaḥ sad-dharma-puṇḍaríka-sútra, and may be roughly Englished, 'Glory (to the) efficient-means-lotus sútra.' It is an invocation to the great metaphysical text-book of Northern Buddhism, the Sad-dharma-puṇḍaríka or *Le lotus de la bonne loi*, as translated by Burnouf, which was taken by the Japanese Nichiren as the starting point in founding his sect. There is another common prayer, *Namu amida Butsū*, which is not a translation, but an imitation of the sound of the Sanskrit phrase, Namo 'mita buddha, 'Hail! immeasurable Buddha!' Here I beg to be allowed to express my obligations to the Japanese gentlemen who, with the willing kindliness of their nation, have been good enough to assist in elucidating many of my difficulties. It would be a pleasure, were it permissible, to mention their names.—I. O'N.

a few inches above the rest of the floor, and which is regarded as the place of honour—his reverence took his seat at the table, and adjusted his robes; then tying up the muscles of his face into a knot expressive of utter abstraction, he struck the bell upon the table thrice, burnt a little incense, and read a passage from the sacred book, which he reverently lifted to his head. The congregation joined in chorus, devout but unintelligent; for the Word, written in ancient Chinese,* is as obscure to the ordinary Japanese worshipper as are the Latin liturgies to a high-capped Norman peasant-woman. The priest next recited a passage alone and .... a small shaven-pated boy brought in a cup of tea, thrice afterwards to be replenished, for his reverence's refreshment, and he, having untied his face, gave a broad grin, cleared his throat, swallowed his tea, and beamed down upon us, as jolly rosy a priest as ever donned stole or scarf. His discourse, which was delivered in the most familiar and easy manner, was an *extempore* dissertation on certain passages from the sacred books. Whenever he paused or made a point the congregation broke in with a cry of "Nammiyô!" a corruption of the first three words of the prayer cited above, to which they always contrived to give an expression or intonation in harmony with the preacher's meaning. Vol. II, p. 125.

§ 6. As this book may, perhaps, be taken up by some who are not already familiar with Japanese texts, it is as well to say that the first page of Japanese books takes the place of the last page of ours. Thus, the Japanese portion of the present book begins at the end of the volume and necessitates a reversed pagination. The lines, too, run perpendicularly from the top to the bottom (North to South) of the page, and follow each other from the left to the right (East to West).

§ 7. With the exceptions pointed out in the note to *Ima* (Sermon, p. 1), the sermon is written in Japanese with cursive Chinese characters and Japanese hiragana intermixed. In most instances, the pronunciation of the Chinese character (*i.e.* either the pure Japanese equivalent or the Japanized Chinese pronunciation) is given in hiragana at the side, but this is occasionally omitted, as in the case of the verb *mōsu*, to say, where the Chinese character sometimes stands for *mō* (Sermon, p. 2, line 3), and sometimes for *mōshi* (page 2, lines 6, 7, &c.). *Koto*, thing, *kokoro*, heart, and *hĭto*, man, will also be found without the hiragana (Sermon, p. 9, &c.). The student will be left to detect other instances of these omissions.

§ 8. The student of this book has the advantage of being able to divide his work into two distinct portions, the study of the language and the study of the character. In the first he may confine himself to the English transcription, on which he can work with the aid of the interlinear translation, the notes and the vocabulary, though, if he intends to make solid progress, industrious labour with Aston's Grammar and Hepburn's Dictionary must also be undertaken. The second division of his work will be the learning of the hiragana and katakana writing, and for this he will, syllable by syllable, compare the Japanese text with the English transcription, referring constantly to the tables at pp. viii to xiv. He had better not at first trouble himself with the Chinese characters, or only with the more simple and frequent, such as *koto, hĭto, mōsu, dai, kokoro, &c.*

§ 9. The punctuation of a Japanese text is conspicuous for one of two reasons; either for its absence or for its capriciousness. When

* See the remarks on this subject at p. 1 of the Sermon.

an attempt at punctuation is made, it generally consists of one sign, a small circle,—the same that converts *ha, hi, &c.*, into *pa, pi, &c.*,—placed at the end of a clause to indicate a breathing place. The Japanese are also frequently heedless of the proper division of words, which thus run into each other, or break off in the middle. It has been suggested that their mode of cursive writing is now somewhat in the same condition as the Western mode was in the time of the earliest uncial manuscripts. Taking for instance, at hazard, the second line or column on page 5 of the Sermon, it is found that "shikazaru ga tame nari to mōshite gozarimasŭ. Naruhodo" appears as *shi kazaru* ga tame nari *tomōshi te go zari masŭ. Naruho do.* These difficulties are not slight to a beginner, but when he reaches the point at which he can correctly write down and punctuate a Japanese text in English letters, he may console himself by the reflection that he has made sensible progress.

Errata in the Japanese Text.

§ 10. It should be borne in mind, that moveable type have not hitherto been used generally in Japan, and that books are cut on wooden blocks, each of which contains the matter of two pages, with the title and pagination* in the centre where the pages are folded. As the paper receives an impression on one side only, a thin quality suffices, and the doubling is explained. The woodcutters copy accurately what is put before them, and it may really be said, that many Japanese books give the handwriting as well as the headwork, the manner in its fullest meaning as well as the matter of the author. This also explains the differing appearances of the characters in different books, and the student must not be discouraged should he find that, although he has become tolerably familiar with the hiragana in one publication, he can scarcely read it at a first effort in another. The woodcutting will also to some extent excuse the following inaccuracies, several of which are mentioned only for the assistance of the beginner :—

Page 5, line 1.—The *ka* of *kara* is not well formed.
" 6 " 4.—*Kakkontō.* The *ko* is very bad, more like *ku.*
" 10 " 3.—*Makiye.* The kana is miscut *mataye.*
" 11 " 5.—*To* is more like *ko.*
" 12 " 5.—*Arō (arau).* The *ra* is not at all clear.
" 14 " 8.—*Katachi.* The *ka* is miscut *ha*, and the *ta* is far from clear.
" 15 " 3.—*Inebutte.* The *te* is careless.
" 16 " 8.—*Utsubuite.* Same remark.
" 20 " 4.—The first stroke of *to* is imperfect.

* It is hardly necessary to point out that the pagination always embraces two pages; thus the 14th double leaf of the Japanese text represents pp. 27 and 28 of the interleaves.

Page 27, line 1.—A katakana character is used for *nu*.

" " " 3.—*Shimpai*. The small circle which converts *ha* into *pa* is omitted.

" 29 " 2.—Second *iwaretari*. The *wa* is not well formed.

" " " 3.—*Kakari-udo*. The woodcutter has here made a compromise between *udo* and *hito* (*bito* in composition), and has produced *hido*. See Notes 29 | 3.

Page 31, line 3.—*Kiki* (*ki* with the sign of repetition), is too much like *kiku*.

" " " 9.—*Suru*. The *ru* is not good.

" 32 " 4.—*Iteki*. *Te* is miscut *se*.

" " " 5.—*Kun-shi*. *Shi* is miscut *ku*.

As is generally the case in Japanese books, the nigori sign is frequently omitted. A list of the instances would be tedious. The student will speedily discover the omissions in going over the Japanese text with the transcription.

Transcription of the Japanese Text in English Characters.

§ 11. Hepburn's method of transcription (2nd ed. of his *Dictionary*), a practical compromise between the actual orthography and the pronunciation, has, for the convenience of English-speaking students, been generally followed, although there are one or two points in his method on which difference of opinion exists. To the Introduction to that Dictionary, and the remarks on the syllabary in Aston's Grammars of the Spoken and Written Language, the student is referred for detailed information on the subject of the English transliteration of Japanese, the following observations being necessarily of a general character.

§ 12. *Crasis of Vowel Sounds*. The student should direct his early attention to this point, which presents little difficulty. There is a full table in Hepburn's Introduction. Instances are so incessant as to forbid a separate list here of all those that occur in the present volume, but the formation of such a list will be an admirable exercise for the student; the instances are clearly to be seen by a comparison of the English transcription and the Japanese text. A reference to Hepburn's Table should clear up any doubt. It will merely be stated here, that *au*, *ou*, and *oo* are pronounced and transcribed as *ō*; and *eu* and *eo* as *ō* or *yō*.

§ 13. The aspirates of the syllabary lose their aspiration in the middle of words. *Ha* then becomes *a* or *wa*; *hi*, *i*; *fu*, *u* or *yu*; *he*, *e* or *ye* and *ho*, *o*. Under these circumstances, combination with another similar syllable or with a vowel often occurs, and a crasis is the result, as in the case of combined vowels.

§ 14. *N*, being pronounced *m* before a labial, is so transcribed, as *zembun* (Sermon, p. 1, line 5). The hiragana is *ze-n-ba-n*.

§ 15. The instances of the elision of *tsu* and the doubling of the following consonant in pronunciation are numerous, as :—

Page 2.—	Mo*tsu*tomo	....	mottomo
	Yo*tsu*te	....	yotte
	I*tsu*shin	....	isshin
Page 3.—	Hi*tsu*ken	....	hikkyō
	Shi*tsu*ta	....	shitta
	Ka*tsu*koutou	....	kakkontō
	I*tsu*tai	....	ittai
	&c.		&c.

In such words as *yotte* and *shitta*, which represent the spoken abbreviations of *yorite* and *shirita*, the spelling with *tsu* is erroneous and obscures the real origin of the words. Although the abbreviations correctly represent the colloquial sounds, such words should properly be written and read as *yo-ri-te*, *shi-ri-ta*.

The transcription is divided by upright strokes (|) to indicate the commencement of each column of the Japanese text.

§ 16. As to pronunciation, natives of Japan had better, if possible, be consulted, but it may be said that the mode of transcription here adopted is a fair phonetic help to Englishmen. The vowels have, to speak roughly, the continental value, and long and short vowels are frequent. The long sign (¯) denotes that the vowel retains its sound, but that that sound is lengthened. The short sign (˘) denotes that the sound is so shortened as sometimes to be almost lost altogether, as in *shĭta*, *shĭka*, which are pronounced almost *sh'ta*, *sh'ka*, and *aisatsŭ*, *fŭta*, *aranŭ*, *sŭkoshi*, *kitsŭne*, which are pronounced almost *aisats'*, *f'ta*, *aran'*, *s'koshi*, *kits'ne*. Double consonants must be carefully dwelt on, as *chĭyotto* and *shitta*, pronounced *chŏt-to*, *sh't-ta*. The sound of *hi* before *t* at the commencement of a word should certainly be picked up from a native. It resembles *sh'* expired forcibly with a minimum of sibillant sound.

§ 17. The literal translation is literally as literal as it could be made. It is feared that the endeavour to adhere as closely as possible to each sentence and even to each clause of the Japanese, and so to give real help to the careful student, has in places left the English in a rather puzzling shape. In the more glaring instances of this nature an explanatory note has been added.* But faithful as the translator has endeavoured to be, the Japanese idiom is so constantly the very reverse of the English, that he has had to call in the auxiliary aid of an interlinear gloss giving the meaning of the majority of words. When the same word occurs several times in a page, the gloss has not always been repeated. Where it was found wholly impossible to translate the

* There is also an excellent and more popular translation of three of Kiu-Ō's Sermons, including that here edited, in Mitford's interesting and valuable "Tales of Old Japan."

Japanese into literal English with any hope of being understood, a note supplies the key. Some of the notes* may be thought trivial, but this is perhaps, from the student's point of view, a fault on the right side. The vocabulary does not pretend to do more than give the signification borne by each word as used in the Sermon, with such elucidation as seemed necessary. The explanation of the various tenses of the verb should be of use to the beginner, who is advised to lose no time in mastering the Tables of the Verbs in Aston's Grammar of the Spoken Language.

The Iroha or A.B.C.

§ 18. The Iroha comprises the 48 sounds which form the Japanese syllabary, arranged in the order which they take in a sort of doggrel verse into which they have been tortured to assist childish memory. It is the A.B.C. taught in the Japanese infant schools, and is contained in the following tables, pp. x to xiv. The first column in each page gives the English sounds of the syllables, the second gives, inscribed in small circles, the corresponding stiff katakana characters, with the Chinese square characters from which they are taken. The remaining columns contain a selection from the cursive hirágana characters, with the Chinese characters from which they are derivations. An endeavour has been made to arrange the hiragana characters in the order of their most frequent occurrence; those in the first column being generally far more frequently met with than others.

§ 19. The more scientific arrangement of the syllabary given at p. viii is usually preferred to the Iroha by native scholars. It follows the vowel sounds *a, i, u, e, o*, and is here confined to the katakana. The three characters which have circles drawn round them were perhaps never in general use, and it is probable that they have been introduced by Japanese systematic writers on grammar to fill up the breaks which were found to exist in arranging the syllables in this tabular form. On the opposite page (ix) the table is reproduced in English letters. It will be observed that the *N* final is wanting in this table, but it will be found (in the circle) at the end of the Iroha tables, p. xiv.

§ 20. With these introductory remarks I commend my First Japanese Book to the indulgence both of the scholar and of the student.

War Office, February 1874. I. O'N.

* The references in the Notes (and in the Vocabulary to the Notes) are to the columns of the Japanese text. Thus the Note "To [9]" at p. 22 of the Sermon refers to *to* in the 9th column of the opposite Japanese page, and "Notes 8 | 3" under Tonami in the Vocabulary refers to a note regarding that word where it occurs in column 8, page 8, of the Sermon.

10.	9.	8.	7.	6.	5.	4.	3.	2.	1.	
ワ	ラ	ヤ	マ	ハ バ	ナ	タ ダ	サ ザ	カ ガ	ア	五十連音韻圖
井	リ	(レ)	ミ	ヒ ビ	ニ	チ ヂ	シ ジ	キ ギ	イ	
(ウ)	ル	ユ	ム	フ ブ	ヌ	ツ ヅ	ス ズ	ク グ	ウ	
ヱ	レ	(エ)	メ	ヘ ベ	ネ 子	テ デ	セ ゼ	ケ ゲ	エ	
ヲ	ロ	ヨ	モ	ホ ボ	ノ	ト ド	ソ ゾ	コ ゴ	オ	

ン

This table gives the katakana characters arranged according to the vowel sounds, *a*, *i*, *u*, *e*, *o*, see § 19, p. vii. The figures serve as a key to the English transcription on p. ix, opposite.

10.	9.	8.	7.	6.	5.	4.	3.	2.	1.	
wa	ra	ya	ma	ha ba	na	ta da	sa za	ka ga	a	‡ Go-
i*	ri	(yi)	mi	hi bi	ni	chi ji	shi zhi	ki gi	i	-ju
(wu)	ru	yu	mu	fu bu	nu	tsu dzu	su zu	ku gu	u	Ren- -in
e†	re	(ye)	me	he be	ne	te de	se ze	ke ge	e (*or* ye)	in
wo	ro	yo	mo	ho bo	no	to do	so zo	ko go	o	dzu

* Originally *wi*. † Originally *we*. ‡ Table of the 50 sounds, arranged in the order of their sounds.

i	イ 伊	い 以	以	伊		
ro	ロ 呂	ろ 呂	呂	路		
ha	ハ 半	は 波	者	八	盤	半
ni	ニ 仁	に 仁	耳	示	示	丹
ho	ホ 保	ほ 保	保	本	本	
he	ヘ 皿	へ 皿	遍	弊		
to	ト 止	と 止	登			
chi	チ 知	ち 知	遅			
ri	リ 利	り 利	利	里	李	離
nu	ヌ 奴	ぬ 奴	怒			

ru	ル 流	る 留	流	類	累	
wo	ヲ 乎	を 遠	遠	乎	越	
wa	ワ 和	わ 和	王			
ka	カ 加	か 加	可	可		
yo	ヨ 與	よ 與				
ta	タ 多	た 太	多	堂	堂	
re	レ 礼	れ 礼	連	麗		
so	ソ 曽	そ 曽	曽	楚	所	
tsu	ツ 門	つ 門	都	津	徒	
ne	子 祢	ね 祢	祢	年		

na	ナ 奈	な 奈	奈	奈	那	那
ra	ラ 良	ら 良	良	羅		
mu	ム 牟	む 武	無			
u	ウ 宇	う 于	宇	宇		
i (yi)	井 韋	ゐ 為	井			
no	ノ 乃	の 乃	乃	農	能	能
o	オ 於	お 於	於	於		
ku	ク 久	く 久	久	具		
ya	ヤ 也	や 也	也	也	屋	
ma	マ 万	ま 末	万	万	滿	

ke	ケ 介	け 計	化	氣	希	
fu	フ 不	ふ 不	婦	布		
ko	コ 己	こ 己	古	故	許	
ye	エ 延	え 衣	盈	要		
te	テ 天	て 天	天	亭	弖	
a	ア 阿	あ 安	阿			
sa	サ 散	さ 左	佐	散	左	
ki	キ 幾	き 幾	幾	起	支	支
yu	ユ 勇	ゆ 由	由	由	遊	
me	メ 女	め 女	免			

Note:—At p. xiii the encircled katakana character given for *ye* is perhaps erroneous. It ought perhaps rather to be the fourth character given under the figure 1 at p. viii, denoted as "*e* or *ye*" on p. ix. But in modern times much confusion has arisen between the aspirated and unaspirated vowel characters, and their indiscriminate use is often perplexing to the beginner.

VOCABULARY.

ERRATA AND ADDITIONS.

In the Vocabulary:—

P. 7;—**Kudasare.** This is the root and imperative of the auxiliary verb *kudasaru*, equivalent in meaning to *nasaru*, but more honorific.

P. 7;—**Kudasarimase.** *Dele* comma after "deign."

P. 11;—**Nasare.** This is the root and imperative of the honorific auxiliary verb *nasaru.*

P. 16;—Insert the following:—**Udo,** see *Kakari-udo.*

P. 18;—**Yotte.** For "thing named" read *saying.*

In the Sermon:—

P. 1, line 2; p. 3, line 9 and Notes, p. 3, line 10;—for "**Shittsū**" read **Shitsū.**

P. 26, line 3;—for "**Kake de**" read **Kakete.**

P. 30, line 4;—**No** (twice) means 'or' and is not for *mono.*

P. 31, note to **Gozarimashō**;—for "implicates" read *implies.*

Vide also *Errata* at the end of the Sermon.

VOCABULARY.

A.

Abunage, danger ; *-ge* is a termination which converts adjectives into abstract nouns. Notes, 20 | 9.

Achira, there (3rd person). Notes, 24 | 3. *Achira de wa*, on that side. See *Kochira* and *Sochira*.

Adzukaru, to be concerned with.

Aisatsŭ, reply, mediation. Notes, 30 | 1.

Aji, taste. Notes, 32 | 6.

Aki, autumn.

Aki, clear, empty.

Akiraka, bright.

Aku, bad. *Aku-shin*, a bad heart ; *aku-gin*, bad money ; *gin* = *kin* with the nigori in composition. Notes, 20 | 2, 4.

Akubi, yawning.

Amari, too much.

Anata, you (polite). Aston, § 15. Notes, 27 | 2.

Ano, that. Aston, § 18. Demonstrative adjective pronoun ; possessive of *are*. *Ano hito*, that man ; *lit.*, the man of that.

Aranŭ, neg. of *aru*. See *Kurushik'aranŭ*.

Arawaremasuru, honorif. form of *arawareru*.

Arawareru, to become manifest.

Arawaruru, Western form of *arawareru*.

Arazu, neg. of *aru*.

Are, that ; pro. (3rd pers.) See *Kore* and *Sore*. Aston, § 16.

Areba (cond. of *aru*), if there be.

Aredomo (concess. of cond. of *aru*), although it be.

Ari, root of *aru*.

Aritagaru, to be desirous (?). For *aritaki aru* (?). Notes, 14 | 5.

Arō, fut. of *aru*. Has a condit. meaning at times, and then = may be, probably is. Notes, 12 | 2.

Arōte, having washed, or washing. Western form of *araite*, part. of *arai* (1st conj.), to wash.

Aru (1st conj.), to be. *Aru hito*, a certain man. *Aru koto* or *aru mono*, an existing thing. *Aru tokoro*, a certain place. Notes, 23 | 9.

Aruji, master.

Ashi, leg. *Ashi-oto* (foot-sound), footstep. Notes, 16 | 7.

Ashi, bad.

Ashiki, bad. Written form. Notes, 20 | 3.

Ashirai, treatment.

Ata ! an interjection.

Atari, root of *ataru*, to hit the target. Notes, 11 | 7.

Ate, root of *ateru* (2nd conj.), to aim at.

Ato, after.

Atokara (after-from), subsequently.

Atte (for *arite*), having been or being. Part. of *aru*. *Atte-mo*, even if it be or were.

Awo-suji, veins apparent through the skin. *Awo*, blue, green, or pale : *suji*, line, vein.

B.

Bakari, only, about.

Ban, evening.

Ban, 10,000.

Beni-sashi-yubi (vermilion — to apply — finger), the third finger. *Sashi*, root of *sasŭ* (1st conj.), to stick on. The vermilion is for the lips. Notes, 2 | 7.

Benjimashita, polite past tense of *benzuru* (irreg. verb), to explain ; *suru*, to do, taking the nigori in compos. Notes, 2.

Bentō, a pic-nic box.

Biyō, disease.

Bu, a fractional part. Originally a tenth. Aston, § 28. Notes, 8 | 4.

Buta. See *Suzuri-buta*.

C.

Chi, blood. Notes, 26 | 8.
Chigai, root of *chigau*. Used as a noun = difference.
Chigau (1st conj.), to be different from.
Chigōte, differing or having differed. Western form for *chigaite*, part. of *chigau*.
Chikagoro (near-time), recently. *Goro* = *koro* with the nigori in compos.
Chikara, strength, *forte*.
Chisai, small.
Chito or **Chitto**, a little, slightly. Notes, 12 | 1.
Chiyotto, slightly.
Chō-men (book-face), ledger.
Chōnin, merchant.
Chōshi, porcelain *sake*-bottle. Notes, 16 | 8.
Chu-ya (day-night) night and day, continually.
Chu-yō (middle-important). The second book of Confucius. Notes, 32 | 4.

D.

Dai (*ōki*), great.
Dai-dokoro, kitchen. *Dokoro* = *tokoro*, place, with the nigori in compos.
Damatte, having been or being silent (for *damarite*), part. of *damaru* (1st conj.), to be silent, to endure.
Danna dono (master, Mr.), the master. Equivalent to *M. le maître*.
Dashi, root of *dasu* (1st conj.), to put out. Trans. of *deru*. In compos. see *Kiyoro*. Notes, 8 | 2, 9.
De, the particle which serves to mark the predicate. Notes, 2, 3, 12 | 2, 14 | 4. Often used elliptically for *de atte*. Notes, 10 | 3. 26 | 1, 27 | 3, 4, 30 | 4.
De, in, with, by means of, at. Aston, § 11. Notes, 11 | 7.
Dekimasenū, honorif. neg. of *dekiru*.
Dekiru (2nd conj.), to be able.
Dekite, being, or having been able. Part. of *dekiru*.
Demasuru, honorif. form of *deru*.
Demo (for *nite mo*), even.
Den = *ten*, a great hall, with the nigori. See *Kiyakū-den*.
Deru (2nd conj.), to come out. See *Dashi*.
Dete, coming, or having come out. Part. of *deru*.
Dettchi, apprentice. Notes, 12 | 3, 4.
Dō, how?
Dō mo. Notes, 18 | 8.
Dō yara (how will it be?), what can be the reason? some how or other. Notes, 27 | 9.
Dō-yō (how-fashion), what manner?
Dō-zo, emphatically how? some how or other. Used idiomatically as equivalent to the English word, Please! in making a request. Notes, 33 | 2. See *Yara*, *Yō*, and *Zo*.
Doko ni, where?
Domburi, bowl.
Domo, a plural particle added to nouns. A humble form of expression. Notes, 27 | 5. Aston, § 6.
Dono (contracted, **Don**). A term of polite address, answering to our Mr. or Miss. *Don* is the more familiar.
Dore, which? Aston, § 19.
Dōri, principle.
Dzura, *tsura* with the nigori. See *Tsura*. Notes, 12 | 1, 3, 4.

F.

Fujin, woman. *Fu*, female; *jin*, man (homo).
Fū-ki (*tomi tattoki*), rich and noble. Notes, 32 | 4.
Fukure-dzura, an ill-tempered face. *Fukure*, root of *fukureru*, to be swollen. See *Dzura*.
Furū, anciently.
Fusho-busho ni, unwillingly.
Fusokū, insufficiency, wanting. *Fu* = not.
Fūta, two. Used immediately before a noun. Otherwise the correct word is *fūtatsū*. Aston, § 25.
Fūtari, two. Numeral for men or women. See *Hitori*. Aston, § 26.
Fūto, suddenly.
Futon, mattress.

G.

Ga, often follows nouns in the nominative case, Notes, 11 | 2; 12 | 4, 5; and is sometimes the sign of the genitive case. *Onore ga hana*, one's own nose. Notes, 11 | 2; 12 | 4, 5; 26 | 1; Aston, § 8. Sometimes has a signification not quite equal to, although resembling, *but*. Notes, 10 | 1, 12 | 4, 5. It is also used as an impressive particle. Notes, 3; 31 | 4.

Gai, harm.

Gaku-mon, learning.

Gata, a polite plural particle which follows nouns to denote distinctly that the plural is meant, or to indicate a class. *Fujin gata*, women generally. Aston, § 6.

Gaten, the act of understanding, comprehension. Notes, 22 | 5.

Gayoi = *kayoi* with the nigori in compos. Notes, 26 | 3.

Gi, righteousness.

Gimmi, examination.

Go, an honorific particle, as *go fujin gata*, women. Notes, 12 | 9, 13 | 3, 14 | 7, 19 | 1, 25 | 8, 27 | 2.

Go, five. **Go-ju** (5×10), fifty.

Go-chisō, feast. The honorif. *go* is indispensable; *chisō* is a running up and down.

Gorōjimase, be good enough to look. *Go*, the honorif. particle; *rō* for *ran*, to see; *ji* (*shi* with the nigori), root of *suru*; *mase*, imperative of *masū*. Notes, 8 | 9, 12 | 3.

Gotoku, like. Written form. Notes, 20 | 5.

Gotoshi, is like, resembles. Written form of verbal adj., including adj. and verb, "to be."

Gozaraba, if there should be. Honorif. hypothetical of *aru*. Notes, 13 | 3.

Gozaredomo, although it be. Honorif. form of *aredomo*.

Gozarimasenū, neg. of *gozarimasū*.

Gozarimasenūka, interrog. of preceding.

Gozarimashite, very honorif. part. of *aru*. See *gozarimasū* and *mashite*.

Gozarimashō, very honorif. fut. of *aru*. See *gozarimasū*. *Mashō*, fut. of *masū*. Notes, 14 | 4, 31 | 4.

Gozarimasū (*go-za-ari-masū*), very honorif. form of *aru*. *Go*, honorif.; *za* (= *sa* with the nigori), place; *ari*, root of *aru*, and *masū*.

Gozarimasuru, same as the preceding, with the addition of *suru*, as an aux.

Gozarō, honorif. form of *arō*. Notes, 13 | 3.

Gozaru, honorif. form of *aru*. When used as a noun, translate "the being."

Gozatte, honorif. form of *atte*.

Gwamme = *kwamme* with the nigori.

H.

Haa! an interjection.

Hadzu, necessity. Notes, 5.

Hadzukashii, shameful (adj. form).

Hadzukashū, ashamed (adv. form).

Haha, mother. *Haha-oya* (mother-parent), mother.

Haisai, consultation.

Haji, shame.

Hajime, beginning. Root of *hajimeru*, to begin.

Haka, vulg. pron. of *hoka*. Notes, 16 | 2.

Hakonda (for *hakobita*), the having carried. Past tense of *hakobu* (1st conj.), to carry, used as a noun.

Hakujō, to confess. Notes, 23 | 1.

Hambun, half. Aston, § 28.

Hana, flower. Notes, 9 | 8.

Hana, nose. *Hana-suji* (nose-line), profile of the nose. *Hana-uta*, see Notes, 18 | 6

Hanahada, very much. *Hanahada motte* (very much taking), very. An adverbial phrase. Notes, 13 | 5.

Hanarenū, neg. of *hanareru*, to get away from, to diverge, to separate, to err.

Hanasareru, pot. or pass. of *hanasū*, to speak. Notes, 27 | 1.

Hanashi, story, talk. Root of *hanasū*, to speak, used as a noun. Notes, 23 | 5.

Hanki, half a year.

Hara, belly. *Hara wo tate* (setting up the belly), working one's self into a rage. Notes, 14 | 2. *Hara no tatsū*, the becoming angry. *Hara tatsū*, to fly into a passion. Notes, 8 | 9, 17 | 1. *Hara no uchi no yugami*. Notes, 22 | 9.

Hare, imperative of *haru*, to spread, to stretch.

Hashi, beginning, end. Notes, 28 | 6.

Hashira, pillar.

Haya, soon.

Hayaku, quickly.

Haye-giwa, the hair-line (on the forehead). *Haye*, root of *hayeru*, to grow; *giwa* (= *kiwa* with the nigori), border.

Hayenū, neg. of *hayeru* (2nd conj.), to grow.
Hayō (for *hayaku*), quickly.
Hebi, snake.
Henji, answer.
Heru, to decrease. *Ki* (spirit) *no heru*, to lose heart.
Higana, daily.
Hiiki, to take any one's part, to be partial. Notes, 30 | 1.
Hiita, past tense of *hiku*.
Hiite, drawing or having drawn. Part. of *hiku*. Notes, 6, 8 | 1.
Hikayete, holding or having held. Part. of *hikayeru*, to hold, keep, stop.
Hiki-akete, pulling open or having pulled open. Part. of *hiki-akeru*. *Hiki*, root of *hiku*; *akeru*, to open.
Hiki-oi, debt.
Hikkiyō, after all, in short, at all, entirely.
Hiku, to draw or pull. Notes, 8 | 1.
Hine-kuri-mawashite, twisting or having twisted round. *Hine-kuri*, to twist; with part. of *mawasū*, to turn round.
Hin-sen (*madzushiki iyashī*), poor and mean. Notes, 32 | 4.
Hitai-guchi (forehead, mouth). *Guchi* = *kuchi* with the nigori. The compound word simply means forehead, the *guchi* being a vulgar suffix. Notes, 11 | 1.
Hitasura ni, wholly.
Hito, man (*homo*). *Otoko* = *vir*. *Hito* is sometimes used in the sense of 'mankind,' and also, like the French *autrui*, in the sense of 'others.'
Hitonami (*nami*, ordinary), usual type of man, general run of men.
Hito-sashi-yubi (man, to point, finger), the index. *Sashi*, root of *sasū*.
Hitori, one person, alone. Numeral for men or women. Notes, 30 | 3. Aston, § 25.
Hitotsū, one. When used before a noun, the *-tou* is dropped, as *hito kire*, one slice. Aston, § 25.
Hiyōshi, measure (in music), concord, harmony.
Hiyōshi ni, pat upon that. Notes, 16 | 8.
Hizagashira, knee-cap. *Gashira* = *kashira* head, with the nigori in compos.
Ho, a sail.
Hōbari, root of *hōbaru*, to stuff into the mouth. *Hō*, cheek; *bari*, root of *haru*, to stretch, with the nigori. Notes, 16 | 4.
Hōbeta, cheek. Vulgar; *hō* is correct. Notes, 11 | 4.
Hodo, quantity, size. Has also an idiomatic signification. Notes, 5. *Kore hodo made* (this quantity, as far as), so much. Notes, 14 | 4, 22 | 6.
Hoka, other. Notes, 17 | 3. *Hoka ni*, without, outside.
Hokku, a kind of Japanese poetry, the measure of which is shorter than *uta*. Notes, 24 | 3, 4.
Hokuchi, moxa. *Kīu* seems to be the blister caused by the moxa, but there is some confusion about this, perhaps owing to the fact that we ourselves use *blister* for both that which is applied and its result. See Hepburn: *Kīu* and *Yaito*. Our word moxa comes from *Mo kūsa*, Mo plant, the *Artemesia Chinensis*, from the dried leaves of which the tinder for the moxa is prepared. Hepburn only gives the meaning 'tinder' for *hokuchi*. See Sermon, p. 6.
Hombuku, recovery. *Hon*, original, and *fuku*, to return; to return to one's original state of health.
Hon, true, real, original. Notes, 10, 5. *Hon ni*, truly.
Hon-gi, true-false. See Sermon, p. 20 | 7.
Hon-shin, original heart, conscience. This indicates a belief the reverse of that in Original Sin.
Hon-sen, *pièce de resistance*. *Hon*, chief, original; *sen*, dish, little table. Notes, 8 | 1.
Horu, to dig, to scoop.
Hō-shin, diverged heart; the heart which has become perverted from the true path. Notes, 2.

I.

I, meaning, opinion, thought.
Ibōta, past tense of *ibou*, to suppurate.
Ichi-do (one-time), once.
Ichi-nichi (one-day), the whole day.
Idzure, who, where. Notes, 29 | 5. *Idzure mo*, every one, all, wheresover, on all sides.
Ii, root of *iu*. Notes, 2.
Ii-awasete, part. of *ii-awaseru* (to speak, to cause to meet), to consult, to plan.

Ii-dako, cuttle-fish (cooked). *Ii*, boiled rice; *dako* = *tako*, cuttle-fish, with the nigori. Notes, 16 | 5.
Ikari, rage.
Ikken (for *ichi ken*), one house. Notes, 5.
Ikkō (for *ichi kō*), wholly.
Ikon, grudge.
Ima, now.
Imashō, fut. of *imasŭ*.
Imasŭ, honorif. form of *iru*, to be. *I*, root of *iru*, and *masŭ*, honorif. aux. verb, "to be."
Imasureba, when I am; condit. of *imasŭ*.
I-nebutte, part. of *i-neburu*, to doze. *I*, root of *iru*, to remain, and *neburu*, to doze.
Ingiyō, seal. Notes, 29 | 2.
Ippan (for *ichi han*), on the whole, as a whole.
Ireba, condit. of *iru*, to be.
Iri, root of *iru*, to enter. Notes, 17 | 7.
Iri-ai (to enter, to meet), twilight.
Iro, colour, and *fig.*, appearance, variety. *Iro-iro*, (adv.) in endless ways. ASTON, § 6. *Iro kaye shina kaye*, Notes, 14 | 5.
Iru, to be, to remain, to exist.
Isha, doctor.
Ishu, meaning.
Issai (for *ichi sai*, one cut), trifling portion. With a neg. means, 'in no way.' Notes, 24 | 6.
Isshin (for *ichi shin*, one body), the body.
Isshō (for *ichi shō*, one life), life-long.
Isso, see Notes, 29 | 8.
Itami, pain. Notes, 3.
Itashi, root of *itasŭ*. *Itashi-kata* (side), a method of effecting. Almost always used with a neg., as in the phrase *itashi-kata nai*, there is no help for it.
Itashimasenŭ, neg. of *itashimasŭ*.
Itashimashita, past tense of *itashimasŭ*.
Itashimasŭ and **Itashimasuru** } honorif. forms of *itasŭ*. Notes, 23 | 1.
Itashita, past tense of *itasŭ*.
Itashite, part. of *itasŭ*.
Itashitō for *itashitaku*, would like to do.
Itasŭ, to do; more polite than *suru*.
Iteki, barbarian.
Itowadzu, neg. pres. of *itou*, to care.
Itta (for *irita*), past tense of *iru*, to enter. Notes, 10 | 4.
Ittai (for *ichi tai*, one body), generally, wholly, altogether.
Itte (for *ikite*), part. of *iku*, to go.
Iu, to say or call. *To iu ni*, Notes, 3.
Iuta, past tense of *iu*.
Iutara (for *iutareba*), if he had said. Condit. past tense of *iu*. Notes, 12 | 2, 13 | 4. ASTON, § 50.
Iute, part. of *iu*. See *To*.
Iwaku. See Notes, 1.
Iwaretari, (freq. of *iwareru*, pass. of *iu*), sometimes being said.
Iwasazu, neg. of caus. of *iu*. Notes, 28 | 9, 29 | 4.
Iya, distasteful.
Iya! an exclamation, = perhaps, to Ah! or Oh!
Iya-iya! an exclamation of dissent. Notes, 27 | 1, 28 | 3, 4.
Iyagaru, to dislike.
Iye, house. *Iye-iye*, different houses. ASTON, § 6.
Iye-iye! an exclamation of dissent.
Iyeba, if or when he says; condit. of *iu*.
Izen, former.

J.

Ja, is, or are. Western dialect for *de aru*, the verb, to be, with the particle which marks the predicate.
Ja, sometimes for *de wa*. ASTON, § 11.
Jama, obstacle.
Jibun, period. Notes, 27 | 9.
Jiki-ni, soon. Notes, 19 | 3.
Jin, benevolence.
Jin, heart. *Shin* with the nigori in compos. See *shin*.
Jin-yokŭ (man-greed) greed.
Jitokŭ, (*midzukara yeru*), to understand naturally.
Jitsu-ni, truly, really.
Jō, nature, feelings.
Ju (*chu* with the nigori), within. Often used as a loose plural like *ra*. Gives a more general meaning to an adverb, as *soko*, there, *sokora*, there (more indefinite), *sokora-ju*, thereabouts.
Jū, ten.
Ju-bako (to pile up, box), nest of boxes. *Ju* is Chinese; *bako* = *hako* with the nigori.

K.

Ka, an interrog. particle. Notes, 9 | 7.
Kagami, mirror.
Kagande (for *kagamite*), being or having been bent. Part. of *kagamu*. Notes, 1.
Kage, shadow, help, protection. Notes, 25 | 2, 26 | 2, 7.
Kakaranū, neg. of *kakaru*, to have to do with, to affect.
Kakaredomo, although it affect, concess. of condit. of *kakaru*.
Kakari-udo, hanger-on. The name given in Japan to those who go down in the world, and then come to live with their relations. *Kakari*, root of *kakaru*, to be hooked to, and *udo*, man, sometimes applied to visitors instead of *hito*. Notes, 29 | 3.
Kakatte, part. of *kakaru*, to be connected with. Has an idiomatic signification, as *hiyōshi ni kakatte*, in chorus. Notes, 30 | 5.
Kakawatta, past tense of *kakawaru*, to relate to.
Kake, root of *kakeru*, to hang up.
Kakemasenū, polite neg. of *kakeru*, to be imperfect.
Kakkontō, an infusion of *kakkon*, "a kind of medicine." Hepburn.
Kaku, to scratch.
Kaku, thus. Notes, 20 | 5, 33 | 1. See *To-kaku*.
Kaku, angle, corner.
Kakuretaru, that which is hidden. Written form; the *-ta-* is that of the past tense. Notes, 17 | 3.
Kakusaremasenū, polite neg. of *kakusareru*, to be hidden (by some one). *Kakusū*, to hide (*cacher*); *kakureru*, to remain concealed (*se cacher*); *kakusareru*, to be hidden (*être caché*). Notes, 17 | 4.
Kakusareru, used as an adj., hideable. See preceding. Notes, 17 | 4.
Kamaboko, a baked hash of fish.
Kamai, root of *kamau*, to care.
Kami-shimo (upper-lower), coat and trousers, ceremonial dress, costume.
Kan, hot, said only of hot *sake* (*sake no kan*).
Kanai (house-inside), family. *Kanai no mono* (person of the family), wife. Notes, 25 | 4, 29 | 6, 7. *Kanai-dzure* (family-company), members of the family; *dzure* = *tsure* with the nigori. Notes, 29 | 3.
Kanashimi, sadness. *Kanashi*, root of adj., sorrowful; *-mi*, termination which converts adjectives into nouns. Notes, 17 | 5.
Kanashiu (for *kanashiku*), sorrowful.
Kane, money. *Kane no oru*, those who have money, the rich. *Kane no nai*, the poor.
Kangayete, part. of *kangayeru*, to reflect.
Kanshaku, rage.
Kanyō, essential. *Yō*, hinge.
Kara, because, from, in consequence of. Notes, 28 | 3, 4, 8.
Karada, body.
Karasū, crow (*corvus*).
Karisome, trifle, bagatelle.
Kari-uke (to hire, to receive), to engage; root form.
Karu-ga-yuye-ni (in the reason of thus), wherefore.
Karui, light, unimportant.
Kata, quarter, side. *Hōbeta no kata ye*, towards the cheek. See *Itashi* and *Maye*.
Katachi, outward appearance, form. Notes, 9 | 7.
Kata-de-iki (shoulder-from-breath), gasping for breath.
Kata-ginu (shoulder-silk), that part of the dress which is on the shoulders, coat; same as *kami*. *Ginu* = *kinu* with the nigori.
Kata-hashi-kara, see Notes, 28 | 6.
Katajikenō, grateful, obliged: *-nō* for *naku*.
Katana, sword.
Katawara, side, beside that. Notes, 28 | 3, 4.
Kata-yotte (side-approaching), on one side, crooked.
Kawaigari (root), to tend affectionately, to nurse.
Kawo, face. Notes, 12 | 1, 4.
Kaye, change. *Iro kaye*, *shina kaye*. Notes, 14 | 5.
Kayeri, root of *kayeru*.
Kayeru, to return.
Kayeshimashō, honorif. fut. of *kayeru*, caus. of *kayeru*.
Kayette, part. of *kayeru*. Idiomatically, on the contrary. Notes, 32 | 9
Kayoi, root of *kayou*, to resort. Notes, 26 | 3.
Kayō-ni, thus, in this manner.
Kayumi, itching.
Kaze, wind. **Kaze hiita** (wind-drawn), caught cold. Notes, 6.
Kazu (*o kazu*), vegetables, or "kitchen," eaten with the rice. Notes, 11 | 7.
Keiko, practice; in the sense of study, education.
Ken, house. Also the numeral for houses, see *Ikken*. Notes, 5.
Kerai, servant.

Ketsŭkare, an insulting aux. verb, the opposite of *kudasare*. Very vulgar. Notes, 12 | 6.
Ki, mind, spirit. Notes, 13 | 2, 20 | 9. *Ki no heru* (to decrease), to lose heart.
Kigen, temper.
Kiitara (for *kikitareba*), if he should hear. Condit. of *kiku*.
Kiite (for *kikite*), part. of *kiku*.
Kiki, root of *kiku*. *Kiki ni*, in order to hear. Notes, 23 | 8.
Kiki-hadsushita, past tense of *kiki-hadsusu*, to miss hearing.
Kikoyesu, neg. root of *kikoyeru*, to be audible.
Kiku, to hear. *Kiku ni*, in (whilst) hearing. Notes, 23 | 8.
Kimyōna, wonderful. Notes, 19 | 2.
Kin-gin, gold and silver.
Kin-nen, recent years.
Kirai, root of *kirau*, to dislike, to hate.
Kire, root of *kireru*, pass. of *kiru*, to cut. Taken as a noun = slice.
Kita, past tense of *kuru*.
Kite, part. of *kuru*.
Kitsui, violent, severe.
Kitsŭne, fox. Notes, 6.
Kiu, the blister caused by a moxa. See *hokuchi*.
Kiu-sokŭ (*iki wo yasumu*), resting. Notes, 33 | 3.
Kiyakŭ, guest. *Kiyakŭ-den*, guest room. *-den* = *ten*, a large hall, with the nigori in compos.
Kiyō-kun, instruction. *Kun* = explanation.
Kiyoro-tsuki-dashi, to roll the eyes. Notes, 8 | 2, 15 | 9.
Ko, son, child.
Ko, little. *Ko-bachi*, a little bowl. *Bachi* = *hachi* with the nigori.
Kochi, here, hither. *Kochi domo*, I, we. *Domo* is a plural particle.
Kochira, here, hither (1st person). *Kochira de wa*, on this side. See *Achira* and *Sochira*.
Koi, imperative of irreg. verb *kuru*.
Koitsŭ (for *kono yatsŭ*), this fellow. Opprobrious; used also vulgarly and familiarly for *kore*. Notes, 13 | 4, 16 | 1, 3, 6.
Koka, the old poetry of Japan.
Koko ni, here.
Kokoro, heart. Notes, 5; 9 | 7; 14 | 1. *Kokoro-bosoi*, sad; *bosoi* = *hosoi*, slender, with the nigori. *Kokoro-dzukai* (obstacle), anxiety. *Kokoro-miru* (to see), to test. *Kokoro-yasui* (easy), intimate. *Kokoro-yete*, part. of *kokoro-yeru*, to think of. See Sermon 8 | 5.

Komatta, annoying, painful. Past tense of *komaru*, to be pained. Notes, 26 | 9.
Komban (for *kono ban*), to-night, this evening.
Ko-mono (small person), apprentice, shopboy.
Konjō (root-disposition), disposition.
Konna (for *kayōnaru*), this sort of.
Kono, this.
Kore, this, here (1st person), see *Are* and *Sore*. ASTON, § 18. *Kore!* here! (*i.e.* come here). *Kore de*, by means of this. *Kore de mo*, notwithstanding this, *nonobstant*. *Kore ga kore* (this is this), it is in this wise. *Kore! kore!* used as an exclamation: Look here! I say! *Kore wa! kore wa!* Ah! I see.
Koro, time. Written language, for *toki*. Notes, 20 | 2; 23 | 7.
Koro-goro (roll-roll), tumbling down (adv.). Notes, 16 | 9.
Koshirayete, part. of *koshirayeru*, to make, to prepare. *Sermon* 28 | 1.
Koso, an adverb of strong emphasis; verily, in very truth, this and no other, thus and thus only. Notes, 9 | 7.
Kosuri-gosuri (rub-rub), rubbing. *Shite*, doing, understood; implies a good deal of rubbing. *Gosuri* = *kosuri*, root of *kosuru*, to rub, with the nigori. Notes, 15 | 6.
Kotayemasuru, polite form of *kotayeru*. Notes, 19 | 3.
Kotayeru, to rebound, to reply.
Koto, thing, affair, matter, term, action. Has an abstract meaning when contrasted with *mono*, which has a more material signification. Notes, 14 | 1, 15 | 1, 18 | 3, 31 | 8.
Koto-ni, particularly, extraordinarily.
Kowai, terrible.
Kōyaku, plaster (surgical).
Koye, voice.
Ko-yubi, the little finger.
Ku, distress, pain.
Kŭ, to eat.
Kuchi, mouth. *Kuchi-gotaye*, "answering back" in a surly manner to one's superiors; "argufying." *Gotaye* = *kotaye*, root of *kotayeru*, to reply, with the nigori. Notes, 18 | 5. See *Hitai-guchi*.
Kuchi-ki (to decay, tree). Notes, 9 | 7, 8.
Kudasare, Notes, 12 | 6.
Kudasarimase, imperative of very honorif. verb *kudasarimasŭ*, to deign to do.
Kumo, spider.
Kuni, country.
Kun-shi, the superior man. See Sermon, 32 | 5.
Kurai, dark.
Kurasŭ, to live. Notes, 23 | 7.

Kure, imperative of *kureru*. Notes, 29 | 2.
Kuremasûredo, although one gives. Polite condit. of *kureru*.
Kureru (2nd conj.), same meaning as *kudasareru*, to deign to do. An honorif. verb.
Kurete, part. of *kureru*. Notes, 28 | 1.
Kuruma-za (wheel-seat), circular seat. Notes, 16 | 5.
Kurushii (for *kurushiki*), distressed, painful.
Kurushik'aranû, painless. *Aranû*, neg. of *aru*, to be. The final vowel of the adjective yields to the first of the verb in compos.
Kurushû, painful.
Kûso, dung.
Kûsûborimasû, polite form of *kûsûboru*, to be blackened by smoke, and fig., to be miserable, wretched. Notes, 29.
Kwamme, see Notes, 28 | 6, 7. Aston, § 106.
Kwan, calamity.

M.

Machigai, mistake.
Machigôte, part. of *machigau*, to differ, to mistake. Notes, 13 | 4, 5.
Machi-wabite, part. of *machi-wabiru*, to be tired of waiting. *Machi*, root of *matsu*, to wait; *wabiru*, to suffer.
Mada, still.
Made, as far as.
Magari, twisting, distortion; root of *magaru*, to bend.
Magatta, past tense of *magaru*. Notes, 9.
Magatte (for *magarite*), part. of *magaru*, bent, twisted, depraved.
Mai, every. Only in compos., as *mai nichi*, every day.
Mairimasû, honorif. form of *mairu*, to go, to enter. *Mairi*, root of *mairu*, and see *masû*.
Maite (for *makite*), part. of *maku*, to roll.
Makasaniya (for *makasaneba*), if one does not entrust. Neg. condit. of *makasû*. Notes, 26 | 6.
Maki-yaki, lit., roll-roast; roots of *maku* and *yaku*. *Tamago* (egg) *no maki-yaki*, omelette.
Maki-ye (gold lacquer, picture), gold lacquer.
Makkuro, very black.
Makoto, truth.
Mamayo, never mind! Notes, 27 | 6, 7.
Manekarete, part. of pass. form of *maneku*, to invite.
Masenû, neg. of *masû*.
Mashita, past tense of *masû*.
Mashite, part. of *masû*.
Masû, honorif. aux. verb, to be. Often suffixed to verbal roots to form a compound polite verb without altering the signification. Aston, §§ 46, 77.
Masuru, another form of *masû*.
Mata, again. Notes, 28 | 3, 4.
Matedomo, although they wait. Concess. of condit. of *matsû*.
Mawaru, to go round. Notes, 8 | 1.
Maye, before. *Maye ni*, in front. *Maye kata* (previous side), formerly.
Mayôta, past tense of *mayô*, to go astray. Notes, 14 | 4.
Me, eye. *Me-bayaku*, quick-eye'dly. *Bayaku* = *hayaku*, with the nigori. *Me no tama*, eyeball.
Menuki, a sword handle ornament. Notes, 11 | 2.
Meshi-taki, cook. *Meshi*, boiled rice; *taki*, root of *taku*, to boil.
Metta-ni, an intensitive adverb; very, excessively, extremely. Notes, 11 | 8.
Mi, the body, self. Notes, 30 | 5.
Mibiiki (self-party), selfishness, egotism. *Biiki* = *hiiki* with the nigori. *Mibiiki migatte*, is an expression used several times in the *Sermon* to denote the self-seeking or "egoism" which warps the mind, as contradistinguished from duty to our neighbour, or "altruism." Notes, 21 | 6, 7.
Mibun (body-part), condition or station in life.
Michi, path, road. Notes, 1.
Michinori (*nori*, law, rule, measurement), distance by road.
Midzu-kagami (water-mirror), surface of water used as a mirror.
Migatte, self-interest. *Gatte* = *katte*, convenience, with the nigori.
Mi-gurushu, painful to see. *Mi*, root of *miru*; *gurushu* = *kurushu*, with the nigori.
Mi-kake-dôshi, to differ from appearance, humbug. *Mi*, root of *miru*; *kake*, root of *kakeru*, to place; *tôshi*, to turn upside down. Notes, 10 | 5.
Mi-kawamuru, to distinguish by sight. *Mi*, root of *miru*; *kiwamuru*, Western form of *kiwameru*, to decide.
Mi-kurabete, comparing by looking. *Mi*, root of *miru*, with part. of *kuraberu*, to compare.

Mimi, ear.
Mina, all. Notes, 33 | 2.
Mi-oboye, root of *mi-oboyeru*.
Mi-oboyeru (2nd conj.), to recognise. *Mi*, root of *miru; oboyeru*, to remember.
Mi-oboyemasuru, honorif. form of preceding. See *Masuru*.
Mi-oboyeta, past tense of *mi-oboyeru*.
Mi-oboyetaru. Written form of past tense of *mi-oboyeru*, with idea of continuance.
Mi-oboyete, part. of *mi-oboyeru*.
Mireba, when he saw, upon his looking at. Condit. of *miru*.
Miru, to see.
Mise, shop.
Mise-kake, outward appearance. *Mise*, root of *miseru*, to show; *kake*, root of *kakeru*, to put forward.
Mise-oki, to display. *Mise*, root of *miseru; oki*, root of *oku*, to put.
Miseru, to show.
Misezu, neg. of *miseru*.
Mi-son-zenŭ, neg. of the following: *-ze* = *se*, neg. base of *suru; -nŭ*, neg. particle.
Mi-son-zuru, to mistake. *Mi*, root of *miru*, to see; *son*, loss; *zuru* = *suru*, to do, with the nigori.
Misureba, if he shows. Condit. of *misuru*, Western form of *miseru*.
Mitomunai, it is unsightly (verbal adj.)
Mi-wake, root of *mi-wakeru*, to distinguish by sight. *Mi*, root of *miru*.
Mi-wakuru. Western form of preceding.
Mi-wasureru, to forget the sight of. *Mi*, root of *miru*.
Mi-yama-gakure (deep-mountain, to be hid), deep mountain recess. *Gakure* = *kakure*, root of *kakureru*, to be hid, with the nigori. Notes, 9 | 7.
Miyemasuru, polite form of *miyeru*, see *Masuru*.
Miye-nikŭ, indistinguishable. *Miye*, root of *miyeru; nikŭ* (in compos.), difficult. Notes, 22 | 3.
Mi-nikŭ, ugly; *mi*, root of *miru*. Notes, 22 | 3.
Miyenŭ, neg. of the following. Notes, 26 | 2.
Miyeru, to seem, to be visible. Formed from *miru*.
Miyete, part. of *miyeru*.
Mo, even, too, already. Sometimes to be translated, 'both,' as *shinrui yenja domo mo*, both relations and connections.
Mo....mo, both... and.
Mō, already.
Mochi, root of *motsu*.
Mochiron (not-argument), of course, clearly certainly.
Mokŭka (eye-under), glance.
Moku-nen (silence-ly) silently.
Mon, crest, cognisance.
Mono, thing, object, person. Sometimes unexpressed and to be understood. Notes, 29 | 5.
Mono-gatari (thing, to relate), story-telling. *Gatari* = *katari*, root of *kataru*, with the nigori.
Mōsaniya (for *mōsaneba*), if I do not speak, neg. condit. of *mōsŭ*. *Mōsa*, neg. base; *ne*, neg. particle; *ba*, if.
Mōsaremashita, honorif. past tense of *mōsu*. *Mashita*, past tense of *masŭ*. Notes, 21 | 4.
Mōsaretaru, a thing told, the saying. Written form. Notes, 19 | 6.
Moshi, if.
Mōshi, the moralist Mencius, whom the Chinese call Meng Tse.
Mōshimashita, honorif. past tense of *mōsŭ*: root of that verb and the past tense of *masŭ*.
Mōshimasŭ, honorif. form of *mōsŭ*; root of that verb and *masŭ*.
Mōshimasŭredo, although called. Root of *mōsŭ* and concess. of condit. of *masŭ*. Notes, 3.
Moshimasuru, same as *mōshimasŭ*. See *Masuru*. Notes, 19 | 1.
Mōshite, part. of *mōsŭ*. Notes, 3.
Mōsu, to call, to say. Notes, 19 | 1. *To mōsŭ*, Notes, 2.
Motadzu, neg. of *motsŭ*.
Moto, origin.
Motomuru, Western form of *motomeru*, to seek.
Mottari, frequentative form of *motsŭ*.
Motte, part of *motsŭ*, to hold, to possess.
Mottomo (adv.), most, very, very much, it is quite true, superlative. *Go mottomo*, quite right! Notes, 29 | 1.
Mufumbetsŭ, want of discrimination. *Mu* is the neg. prefix, = non-.
Mugō, cruel.
Mukō, opposite. Notes, 8 | 2.
Mŭma, horse.
Mŭmei, nameless. *Mŭmei shi*(finger), the third finger. Notes, 3.
Muna, *see* the following.
Mune, breast. Sometimes *muna*, for euphony, as before *ye*. Sermon, 19 | 3.
Muri, wrong, fault. *Mu*, not; *ri*, reason.
Muri-rashi, fault-resembling. *Rashi* = English termination *-ish*; *kodomo-rashi*, child-ish. Aston, § 37.

Muri-yari, reckless. *Yari*, root of *yaru*, to do. Notes, 31 | 8, 9.
Mushin, application, request. Notes, 29 | 2.
Mutsŭkashi, difficult.
Muyō (not-function), the being without an office or function.

N.

Na, name.
Na (for *naru*), used much in compos., as *ōki-na*, *yō-na*, &c.
Nabe, pot, stewpan.
Nado, *et cætera ; see* also Notes, 27 | 4.
Nagame, root of *nagameru*, to look fixedly.
Nagara, whilst. Notes, 15 | 6.
Nagashi-moto, the sink in a scullery. *Nagashi*, root of caus. of *nagareru*, to flow ; *moto*, quarter, direction.
Nai (for *naki*) is not, (adj.), used as neg. of *aru*, to be. Notes, 5. Aston, §§ 37, 62.
Naite, part. of *naku*. Notes, 32 | 9.
Naka, middle ; also the relations subsisting between individuals. Notes, 29 | 7. *Naka-naku*, to the very heart, thoroughly, utterly. Notes, 27 | 4.
Nakanŭ, neg. of *naku*, to cry.
Nakasu, neg. of *naku*, to cry.
Nakimasenŭ, neg. of *nakimasŭ*, polite form of *naku*.
Nakisōna (see *Sōna*), likely to cry. Notes, 24 | 6, 7. *Naki*, root of *naku*.
Naku, adverbial form of *nai*.
Naku, to cry.
Nakuba, if there be not.
Nakutte, not being ; part. of *naku*.
Nambo (for *nanihodo*), how much ? what quantity ? Notes, 17 | 2.
Name-kŭsatta, conceited, impudent. *Nama*, raw ; *kŭsatta*, past tense of *kusaru*, to be rotten. Notes, 12 | 3.
Namida, tear. Notes, 26 | 9.
Nan, difficulty.
Nan (for *nani*), what. Aston, § 19. *Nan de ?* (for what ?) why ? *Nan ja ?* for *nani de aru ?* what is it ? Notes, 15 | 9. *Nan no ?* what ? *Nan to* (that what ?) what ? as in *nan to shite ?* what is he doing ? *nan to iu ?* saying what ? *Nan to !* (an exclamation) well ! well ! what ? Notes, 9 | 6, 12 | 2. *Nan zo*, something. *Nan zo ya*, something or other ; *zo*, emphatic, and *ya*, interrogative particles. Notes, 9 | 2. See *Nani*.
Nan, fut. of *nuru*, written form. Notes, 9 | 8.
Nanatsŭ, seven.
Nangi (difficulty-thing) trouble, woe. *Nangi-banashi*, trouble-talk, twaddling about one's troubles. *Banashi* = *hanashi* with the nigori.
Nani, what ? why ? Aston, §§ 19, 20. Notes, 26 | 7, § 19, 20. *Nani ga*, something ; a detached phrase used in conversation to fill up a pause. Notes, 23 | 8. *Nani-goto mo*, all things soever ; *goto* = *koto* with the nigori. *Nani nari to mo*, be it what it may ; *see* the several words ; *shite*, doing, may be supplied after *to*. *Nani to zo* (emphatically, what ?), by all means. (See *Nan*.)
Nankin, southern capital. *Pekin* (in Japanese *Hok-kin*), northern capital.
Naosō, fut. of *naosu*.
Naosu, to mend.
Nara, for *nareba*. Notes, 31 | 1.
Naranŭ, neg. of *aru*, to be.
Naranŭ, neg. of *naru*. Lit., 'becomes not' ; idiomatically, 'will not do,' 'will not answer'; an important idiom in Japanese ; *Manebaneba naranŭ*, if one does not learn, it will not become, *i.e.*, one must learn. Notes, 16 | 7, 22 | 7, 26 | 6. *Naranŭ koto*, a wrong thing. It is odd that the literal translation is, 'a thing that does not become,' 'an unbecoming thing.' Notes, 18 | 9, 31 | 8, 32 | 2.
Narashi, root of *narasu*, caus. of *naru*, to sound.
Narasu, neg. of *naru*.
Nare, to be (after *koso* in the written language). Notes, 9 | 7.
Nareba, since it is ; condit. of *naru*.
Naredomo, although it be ; concess. of condit. of *naru*. Notes, 26 | 8.
Nari, root of *naru*. Notes, 9 | 8.
Narimasenŭ, polite neg. of *naru*. See *Masenŭ* and remarks on *naranŭ*.
Narimashita, past tense of *narimasuru*. Notes, 23 | 6, 7. See *Mashita*.
Narimashite, part. of *narimasuru*. See *Mashite*.
Narimasuru, polite form of *naru*. See *Masuru*.
Narite, part. of *naru*.
Naru, to be, to become

Naru-hodo (to become, quantity,—*i.e.*, actual amount), really. An idiomatic expression much used; resembles our, Quite so!
Narumai, neg. fut. of *naru* (1st. conj.). This tense is formed from the infin. in the 1st conj., and from the neg. base in the 2nd.
Nasaba, if one caused (something) to become. Hypothetical of *nasu*, caus. of *naru*. Notes, 9 | 8.
Nasare, Notes, 12 | 6.
Nasaremase, polite imperative of *nasaru*.
Nasaremasuredo, although one does, concess. condit. of *nasaremasŭ*.
Nasaremasuru, to do; very honorif. compound verb. Contains *nasaru*, *masŭ*, and *suru*; all meaning, to do. The two first are honorific. Notes, 19 | 2.
Nasarenŭ, neg. of *nasaru*.
Nasareta, past tense of *nasaru*.
Nasarete, part. of *nasaru*.
Nasarimase, same as *Nasaremase*.
Nasaru, to do, to please to do; an honorif. verb. Notes, 19 | 1. Aston, § 78.
Nashi (adj.) used as neg. of *aru*, to be. *Nai* is more common. Aston, § 37.
Natta (for *narita*), past tense of *naru*.
Natte (for *narite*), part. of *naru*.
Naze, why? *Naze nareba* (why, because it is?) *-ba* = *wa*; therefore the phrase is, 'in regard to its being, why?' or, 'why is it?' or, simply, 'why?' Notes, 21 | 7.
Ne, sound. *Shika no ne*, the belling of the stag. *Tori no ne*, the singing of birds.
Nebuka, a kind of garlic.
Nebuke, sleepiness. *Nebu*, from *neburu*, same as *nemuru*, to sleep; *ke*, spirit.
Nejire-dasu, to begin to be twisted. *Nejire*, root of *nejiru*, to be twisted. Notes, 8, 9.
Nen, year. *Nen-nen*, yearly.
Ni, two.
Ni, to, in, or at. It is the particle which is the sign of the dative case or *ni kaku*. Following the root of a verb it means, 'in order to,' as *uke ni*, in order to receive. After the attributive form, on the other hand, it is 'in,' as *iu ni*, in saying. Aston, §§ 9, 64.
Nichi-nichi, every day.
Nigiru, to grasp.
Nin, man.
Ninjō, sword-edge. Sermon, 13 | 8.
Nirami-mawashi, to glare round. *Nirami*, root of *niramu*; *mawashi*, root of caus. of *mawaru*, to go round.
Nite, in. See *Oite*. Notes, 20 | 8.
Niwa, garden.
Niyobō, wife.
No, the particle which is the usual sign of the genitive case, or *no kaku*. When two nouns are in apposition, the Japanese idiom introduces *no* between them; *see* Notes, 6 | 1, 2; 29 | 3. *Meshitaki no o San dono*, Sermon, 10 | 5. *Dettchi no Chōkichi*, Ibid., 10 | 6, 7. *See* also Notes, 10 | 6.
No, has frequently the same signification as *mono*, a thing. Notes, 17 | 9.
Nobashite, part. of trans. verb *nobasu* (1st conj.), to stretch.
Nobinu, neg. of intrans. verb, *nobiru*, to stretch. Notes, 3.
Nogareyō, fut. of *nogareru*, to escape, to avoid. Notes, 32 | 3.
Nokotte (for *nokorite*), part. of *nokoru*, to remain behind, to be left.
Nomi, alone (adv.).
Nukaranŭ, unconscious. *Nu*, not; *karanŭ*, to be disjointed. *Nukaranŭ kawo*, an unconscious face, has a cunning sense; is used of a face that is assumed, or, as we say, put on. Notes, 31 | 2.

O.

O, an honorif. particle largely employed. Notes, 11 | 7, 12 | 9, &c.
Oboshimeshite, part. of *oboshimesŭ*, an honorif. verb, to think.
Oboyemasŭ, honorif. form of *oboyeru*.
Oboyete, part. of *oboyeru*.
Oboyeru, to feel, to think.
Ōgi, fan.
Ogori, prodigality. Notes, 32 | 8.
Oitaru, old. For *oi te aru*, he who is old. Notes, 31 | 4.
Oite (for *okite*) part. of *oku*, to place. *Ni-oite* is the same as *nite*, in. Notes, 20 | 8.
Okashimi, merriment. Root of adj. ridiculous, and *-mi*, termination which converts adj. into nouns. Notes, 17 | 7.
Oki / **Ōki** } large. Notes, 8 | 4.
Okoru, to arise. Notes, 15 | 1.
Oku, back. Notes, 15 | 5.
Omaye, you (familiar). Aston, § 15. Notes 31 | 3.

Omoi, root of *omou*.
Omoi, heavy.
Omoi-tsŭkŭ (to think, to stick) to resolve on, to intend. Notes, 22 | 6.
Omoshiroi, amusing.
Omōte, part. of *omou*. See *To*.
Omou, to think.
Omowadzu, neg. root of *omou*.
Omoyeba, when I think. Condit. of *omou*.
Onaji, same.
Oni, devil.
Onna, woman.
Onore, oneself. You, yourself (in an opprobrious sense). Notes, 12 | 5.
Ore, I. Self-abasing. Aston, § 14.
Orimasŭredo, although one remains. Concess. of condit. of *orimasŭ*, honorif. form of *oru*, to be, to remain.
Osayetsŭ. See *Saitsŭ*.
Ōserareta, past tense of *ōseru*, to say. An honorif. verb used only in quoting the dictum of a sage. Notes, 7.
Oshi-komi, to thrust in. Roots of *osŭ*, to thrust, and *komu*, to put into.
Oshi-narashite, striking an average, taking all together. Root of *osŭ*, to thrust, and part. of *narasŭ*, to level. Notes, 31 | 6.
Oshiye-kata. Mode of instruction. Root of *oshiyeru*; *kata*, side.
Oshiyeru, to teach, to instruct, to inform.
Oshiyete, part. of *oshiyeru*.
Oshiyuru, Western form of *oshiyeru*.
Oshō, priest.
Ōte (for *aite*) part. of *au*, to meet.
Otoko, man (vir). *Hito* = homo.
Ototsui, the day before yesterday. Notes, 17 | 1.
Oya-yubi (parent-finger), thumb.
Oyobu, to come to.

P.

Pachi-pachi, such a noise as is made in 'flirting' a fan, or fiddling with it.

R.

Raku, ease.
Rei, thanks.
Ri, 4,275 yards. Notes, 4.
Ri. See Notes, 25 | 6.
Rinshoku (*oshimu*), parsimonious.
Riyō, both. Notes, 8 | 2.
Riyō, an abstract unit of money, like our 'pound.' At present equal to about one dollar. Notes, 27 | 6.
Riyō-gaye, money-changing. *Gaye* = *kaye*, root of *kayeru*, with the nigori. *Riyō-gaye-ya*, a money changer's shop.
Riyō-ji, medical treatment.
Riyō-ken-chigai, mistake. *Riyōken*, plan, thought, idea, and *chigai*, root of *chigau*, to differ.
Rōjin, old man. Notes, 28 | 9.
Rokŭ, six.

S.

Sa! or **Saa!** an interjection arresting attention. Notes, 25 | 8.
Sadamete, having decided, certainly, surely, doubtless. Part. of *sadameru*, to fix, to settle. *Sadame*, a rule or regulation.
Sai, year (of age). Notes, 25 | 9.
Sai-jō (extreme-upper), first, former, first of all, best.
Saisokŭ, demand, instigation.
Saite (for *sakite*), part. of *saku*, to open (as a flower).
Saitsŭ osayetsŭ, passing the wine-cup. An idiomatic phrase, see Notes, 24 | 4.
Sakadzuki, wine-cup. Notes, 16 | 8.
Sakana, cooked fish.
Sake, a general name for all intoxicating liquors in Japan. *Sake no kan*, hot sake.
Saki, tip, point, end, before. See also *tokui-saki*, Sermon, p. 28, which means, customers.
Sakki, same as the foregoing. *Sakki ni* (in the before), 'ere now.

Sama, appearance. *Sama-zama*, all appearances, all kinds. Notes, 31 | 9.
Sama, gentleman. Notes, 33 | 2.
Samu, cold (root form).
San, three. Notes, 12 | 2.
San-gen (for *san ken*), three houses. ASTON, § 26. Notes, 8 | 3.
San-kaku, three-cornered.
Sari (for *sa ari*), so it is. *Sari-tote(to iute)*, saying that so it is, this being so. Notes, 25 | 9.
Saru (for *sa aru*), such, so. Notes, 19 | 5. *Saru hito*, a certain man. *Saru ni yotte*, in regard to its being so, therefore.
Sasaye, wine-jar.
Sassharu, same as *saseru*, caus. of *suru*.
Sate, now! as in the phrase, 'Now there was a man,' &c. Marks transition.
Sato, village; also a wife's home. *Sato ye kayesu*, to send a wife back to her home, to divorce her. Notes, 29 | 9.
Saye, only.
Sayōna (*na* for *naru*) thus-fashion, to be, such.
Segare, youngster. Said by a father of his son. Notes, 25 | 9.
Sei-soroye, display. *Sei*, to prepare; *zoroye* = *soroye*, root of *soroyeru*, to sit in a row, with the nigori.
Seken, the world. Notes, 4.
Seki, seat.
Semete, at least.
Sen, a thousand.
Sen-ban (1,000×10,000) ten millions. Notes, 13 | 2.
Sen-daku, to wash. *Sen* (Chinese), by itself, means to wash; *arau* is the Japanese equivalent. Notes, 12 | 6, 7.
Seniya (for *seneba*), if he do not. Neg. condit. of *suru*. Notes, 22 | 7.
Senū, neg. of *suru*. Notes, 12 | 6, 7.
Seraruru, pass. of *suru*, used as an honorif. Notes, 13 | 4.
Setsunai, uneasy.
Sewa, trouble. Notes, 12 | 5, 14 | 1. *Sewa ni naru*, to receive assistance.
Sezū (for *sedzu*), not doing. Neg. part. of *suru*.
Shakūshi, a wooden ladle. Notes, 11 | 7.
Shi, finger (Chinese). *Tō*(head) *shi*, index finger; *chu shi*, middle finger; *dai* (great) *shi*, thumb; *shō shi*, little finger. See also *Yubi*, the Japanese word for finger.
Shi, Chinese poetry. Notes .24 | 3.
Shi, four.
Shi, root of *suru*.
Shibura-kobura, lazily.
Shibutoi, sluggish, sullen.
Shichi, seven.
Shika, deer.
Shikareba, if one scold; condit. of *shikaru*
Shikari, root of *shikaru*.
Shikaru, to scold, to reprove.
Shikashi, thus, this being so, but. *Shikashi nagara*, this being as it is, nevertheless, but.
Shikato, firmly, accurately, steadily. Notes, 20 | 1.
Shikatsūberashu, precisely, accurately, finically; *-shu* is for *-shiku*.
Shikazaru, neg. of *shiku*, to resemble.
Shikori, root of *shikoru*, to be engrossed by.
Shimeshi, root of *shimesu*, to instruct.
Shimo, lower; opposed to *kami*. Also, trousers.
Shimpai, anxiety.
Shin, heart. See *aku-shin*, *hō-shin*, *hon-shin*.
Shina, article. *Iro kaye*, *shina kaye*. Notes, 14 | 5.
Shindai, property.
Shingaku (heart-learning), the study of morality.
Shinjutsu (heart-art), heart. The heart and its objects.
Shinrui, blood relation.
Shiranū, neg. of *shiru*. Sermon, 5 | 7.
Shirazu (for *shiradzu*), not knowing. Neg. part. of *shiru*. Notes, 9 | 5.
Shiremasenū, polite neg. of *shireru*.
Shireru, to be known. Intrans. of *shiru*. *Shirareru* is the pass. form.
Shiri, bottom, the back, hips.
Shiri, root of *shiru*. Notes, 5 | 5.
Shirok'arō (for *shiroku arō*) will or may be white. Notes, 10 | 1.
Shirōto-gata (white-man-person), a non-professional.
Shiru, to know. When used as a noun, translate 'knowledge.' Notes, 5 | 5. *Shiru-koto* (circumstance), knowledge.
Shisokū, son.
Shita, past tense of *suru*.
Shita, below. Notes, 28 | 3, 4, 8.
Shite, part. of *suru*. See *To*. Notes, 15 | 6, 20 | 1.
Shite, part. of *Shīru*, to urge. By force, 'right or wrong,' 'whether or no.' See Sermon, 27 | 3, and 32 | 3.
Shitsū, itching and pain. Notes, 3.
Shitta (for *shirita*), past tense of *shiru*.
Shitte (for *shirite*), part. of *shiru*. Sermon, 5 | 6.
Shiutan, lamentation.

Shō, section, sentence, verse.
Shō, little, small.
Shōbai, business.
Shō-ben (little convenience), micturition. *Shō ben tareru*, to micturate. See *Tarete*. *Dai ben* = great convenience.
Shōgai (life-limit), lifelong.
Shōgazake (ginger-sake), ginger cordial, *sake* taking the nigori in compos.
Shō-gin, correct or genuine money, *kin*, money, taking the nigori in compos.
Shōji, sliding shutters consisting of wooden frames covered with paper. Notes, 30 | 8.
Shōjiki, straight, upright, honest.
Shōya (beginning-night), early part of the night.
Shu, a plural particle. *Mise no shu*, the people of the shop.
Shu-jin, Master. Notes, 28 | 1.
Shu-wo, shame. Sermon, 5 | 4.
Soba, beside, near.
Sochira, there (2nd person). See *Achira* and *Kochira*.
Soji, cleansing (noun).
Sōkaye, is it so, indeed? *Sō*, it is thus, it is so; very near the German *so*; *ka*, interrogative particle; *ye* is here a particle with no translateable equivalent.
Sokka, you.
Soko, there. *Soko de*, therewithal, therefore, now.
Sokonemasuru, polite form of *sokoneru*, to spoil.
Sokora, there, *sokora-ju*, thereabouts. *Ju*, = *chu* with the nigori, a plural termination. Notes, 10 | 3.
Sōna (for *sayō naru*), it seems to be.
Sono, that. ASTON, § 18. *Sono ato kara* (that-after-from), thenceforward.
Sō-ō, proportionate, suitable, fit. Notes, 23 | 7.
Sore, that (2nd person). See *Are* and *Kore*. ASTON, § 18. *Sore ni*, that being so, in addition to that. *Sore-zore*, each and every. The second *sore* takes the nigori. Notes, 3 | 4.
Sori, the back of a sword. *Sori-utte*, turning the back of the sword over in the belt so as to be ready to draw. *Utte*, for *uchite*, part. of *utsu*, to strike.
Soro-soro, slowly, gradually.
Sū, an interjection of distress.
Sugata, form, appearance.
Suji, line, vein visible through the skin.
Suki, root of *suku*, to like.
Sūkoshi, slightly, a little.
Sūmi, ink.
Sunawachi, namely, *id est*.
Sureba, if or when one does. Condit. of *suru*. Notes, 14 | 1, 19 | 1, 32 | 2.
Suri-muita, abraded. *Suri*, root of *suru*, to scrape; *muite* (for *mukita*), past tense of *muku*, to skin.
Suru (irreg. verb), to do, to make.
Susūme, root of *susūmeru*, to persuade. Notes, 19 | 1.
Sūtete, having thrown away, rejected. Part. of *sūteru*. *Sūtete-oite*, leaving alone. *Oite*, for *okite*, part. of *oku*, to put. *Sūte* (root) -*oku*, to leave alone.
Sūwatte (for *sūwarite*), part. of *sūwaru*, to squat.
Suzuri-buta, a lacquer tray. Notes, 15 | 7. *Buta* is vulgar; it should be *futa*.

T.

Ta, other. *Ta nashi*, is not other. See *Nashi*. Notes, 1. *Ta-nin* (other-man), stranger.
Tabi, time, occasion. *Hito-tabi*, once.
Tachi-machi, immediately, suddenly. Roots of *tatsū*, to stand, and *matsū*, to wait.
Tachimasuru, polite form of *tatsū*.
Tachi-wadzurai, a chronic malady.
Tada, only.
Tadashite, part. of *tadasu*, to correct, to adjust.
Tadzūne, root of *tadzūneru*, to inquire.
Tagai, both you and I, all of us. *Tagai ni*, mutually. ASTON, § 21. Notes, 14 | 5.
Tagui, kind, class. Notes, 1, 9 | 5.
Tai, great. *Tai-biyō*, a grave disease.
Tai-setsū, important.
Taka, high. *Taka-taka yubi*, the (high-high) middle finger. The second *taka* takes the nigori.
Tama, ball.
Tamago (ball-little), egg. *Tamago no maki-yaki*, an omelette.
Tame, reason. *Tame-ni*, because, on account of, by reason of.
Tamoto, sleeve. From *te*, hand, which becomes *ta* in compos., and *moto*, direction.
Ta-nin (other man), stranger.

Tanomi, root of *tanomu*, to request.
Tanoshimi, pleasure.
Tanoshinde (for *tanoshimite*), part. of *tanoshimu*, to be joyful.
Tanto, plenty.
Taoremasuru, polite form of *taoreru*, to fall; at p. 28 of the Sermon it means 'to become bankrupt.' The kana is *ta-fu*, which would give *tō*, — Introduction to Hepburn's Dictionary, 1st ed., p. xi,— but I have followed p. 458 of the same edition, and p. 34 of its Index, in writing *tao*, which also accords with the pronunciation.
Tare, anyone, who? Notes, 15 | 8.
Tare, root of *tareru*.
Tareru, to drip, to evacuate.
Tarete, part. of *tareru*.
Tataite (for *tatakite*), part. of *tataku*, to knock.
Tatami, floor-mat. Notes, 17 | 1.
Tatanū, neg. of *tatsū*. Notes, 10 | 3.
Tate, root of *tateru*, to set up, formed from *tatsū*.
Tatoye, illustration, example.
Tatsū, to stand, to arise. Notes, 10 | 3, 18 | 1, 27 | 9.
Tatta (for *tachitu*), past tense of *tatsū*.
Tatta, same as *tada*, simply, merely, even.
Tatte (for *tachite*), part. of *tatsū*.
Tei-shu, master, husband.
Ten, a large hall, see *Kiyakū*.
Tenka (heaven-under), the whole nation.
Tenugui, towel. *Te*, hand; *nugui*, root of *nugū*, to wipe.
Terashite, part. of *terasu*, to cause to reflect.
Te-tsudaimasuredo, although he lends a hand. Concess. of condit. of *tetsudaimasuru*, polite form of *tetsudau*. *Te*, hand; *tsudau*, to pass on from one to the other.
To, a particle of which the signification varies. It is frequently employed as a conj., in the sense of 'if,' 'when,' 'as soon as.' It more generally denotes a quotation, or the end of a speech in a dialogue, when it may be rendered 'thus,' as in Milton's "To whom thus Adam—." Notes, 20 | 6. When used as the sign of quotation, there are five verbs, parts of which, generally the participle, have constantly to be supplied in translation, being understood after *to*. They are, in the order of their frequency, *iu*, to say, *omou*, to think, *suru*, to do, *miru*, to see, and *kiku*, to hear. See Notes, *passim*.
To, sometimes means 'that,' as *kane to shiru*, to know that it is money. *Naru*, to be, is here understood before *to*. See Notes, 4, 6, 8 | 8, 20 | 4.
Tō, this.
Togire, root of *togireru*, to suspend. Sermon, 24 | 9.
Tōi, distance, distant. Notes, 1, 4.
Toiki, sigh.
Tokaku, some how or other. See Notes, 27 | 5, 33 | 1.
Toki, time. Notes, 1, 20 | 2, 24 | 5. *Toki ni*, by the bye!
Tokoro, place, spot. Used also for circumstance, occasion. Notes, 16 | 6, 18 | 3, 32 | 8.
Tokui, customer. Notes, 19 | 5. *Tokui saki*, customers. Sermon 28 | 6. *Tokui no hanashi*. Notes, 19 | 5.
Tomari-gake, to stay all night. Root forms of *tomaru*, to stay, and *kakeru*, to set about; the latter with the nigori.
Tonari, neighbour. *To*, door; *nari* (for *narabi*), row. The man whose door is in a row with yours. Notes, 8 | 3.
Tonto, at all. Notes, 24 | 4.
Toreta, past tense of intrans. verb *toreru*, to take oneself away.
Tori-atsūkawanū, neg. of *tori-atsūkau*, to handle. *Tori*, root of *toru*.
Tōri, manner, like.
Toru, to take.
Tosei (*yo watari*), lit. world, to cross,—to pass thro' the world, to live, and thence, livelihood, business.
Tōshi, to turn upside down, see *mi-kake-dōshi*.
Tōshi, distant. Notes, 1.
Tote (for *to iute*), saying that . . . , thus saying. *Nari tote*, saying that it was. Notes, 19 | 5.
Tōtte (for *tōrite*), part. of *tōru*, to pass through from one place to another. Notes, 10 | 2.
Tōzakari (distant, to split), to become distant, to fall away from. Notes, 22 | 1.
Tsuba, the guard of a sword.
Tsugi, next, succeeding.
Tsūgō, circumstance. Sermon, 28 | 5.
Tsuide, course, regular order. Part. of *tsugu*, to join on. *Tsuide ni*, in the course of a narration. Notes, 19 | 4.
Tsuite, part. of *tsuku*. *Kore ni tsuite* (sticking to this), in connection with this. Notes, 19 | 4.
Tsukawareru, to be spent.
Tsukawaruru, Western form of preceding.
Tsūkei, imperative of *tsukeru*, to put on. The imperative (*tsuke*) with *i* added is rare.
Tsukerare, pass. of *tsukeru*, formed from its

root, *tsuke*. Used as an honorif. Notes, 13 | 2.
Tsuketa, past tense of *tsukeru*, to give, trans. of *tsuku*.
Tsukeyō, future of *tsuku*. Notes, 31 | 9.
Tsuki, root of the following. Notes, 8, 2.
Tsuku, to stick.
Tsukuri, root of *tsukuru*, to make.
Tsumamu, to take between the finger and thumb.
Tsumande (for *tsumamite*), part. of *tsumamu*. Notes, 16 | 4.
Tsumuri, head. *Atama* is a commoner word.
Tsuno, horn. Notes, 12 | 7. *Tsuno-dzuki-ai* (of cows), to horn each other. *Dzuki*=*tsuki*, root of *tsuku*, to stab, with the nigori; *ai*, root of *au*, to meet.
Tsuppari, for *tsuki-hari*, root of *tsuki-haru*, to swell out.
Tsura, face. More accurately 'phiz.' Never used but in a bad sense. The correct word is *kawo*.
Tsurai, hard. Notes, 30 | 4.
Tsurō, hard.
Tsū-yō (thorough-fashion), current.

U.

Uchi, the inside. Notes, 22 | 9; also, house. *Uchi-ni*, within, while. Notes, 24 | 9. *Sono uchi ni*, in the inside of that (*i.e.*, what has gone before), meanwhile. Notes, 30 | 6. *Naranū uchi* (inside the not becoming), before it becomes. Notes, 18 | 9.
Uchi-ju (house-middle), the whole family. Notes, 29 | 8. *Ju*=*chu* with the nigori.
Uchi-narashi, to sound by striking (root). Roots of *utsū*, to strike, and of *narasu*, caus. of *naru*, to sound.
Ukami, root of *ukamu*, to float, to swim, Notes, 17 | 6.
Ukemasuru, polite form of *ukeru*. When used as a noun, translate 'the receiving.'
Uke, root of *ukeru*. *Uke ni*, in order to receive.
Ukeru, to receive. *Ukeru ni*, in the receipt.
Uketamawarimashita, polite past tense of *uketamawaru*.
Uketamawaru, to hear, to listen. Notes, 13 | 3. When used as a noun, translate 'the listening.'
Ukete, part. of *ukeru*.
Uketsukeru, to admit of. *Uke*, root of *ukeru*.
Uki-yo-banashi (buoyant-world-talk) gossip. *Banashi* = *hanashi* with the nigori.
Uma, horse. See *mūma*.
Umai, sweet, savory. *Umai mono*, delicacies.
Umarete, part. of *umareru*, to be born.
Umare-tsūki, nature. Roots of *umareru*, to be born, and *tsuku*, to adhere.
Uma-sōna, dainty-like. *Uma* for *umai* in compos. See *Sōna*.
Urami, root of *uramu*, to hate. Notes, 30 | 3.
Ureshigatte (for *ureshigarite*), joyful-feeling, feeling pleased. Part. of *ureshigaru*.
Ureshimi, joyfulness. *-mi*=-ness, termination which converts the root of an adjective into a noun. Notes, 17 | 6.
Ureshi-sōna, joyful-like, pleased. See *Sōna*.
Urotayeta, past tense of *urotayeru*, to be confused.
Ushi, cow.
Uta, Japanese poetry, each stanza of which consists of five lines, containing five, seven, seven, five and seven syllables respectively. *Uta wo yomu*, to compose (*lit.*, to read) poetry. Notes, 9 | 7, 8, 24 | 2, 3.
Utsūbuite (for *utsubukite*), part. of *utsubuku*, to stoop.
Utsūkushik'arō (for *utsūkushiku-arō*) will, or may be, beautiful. *Arō*, fut. of *aru*, to be.
Utsuri, root of *utsuru*, to pass.
Utsūshite, part. of *utsusu*, to copy, to reflect as a mirror.
Utte (for *uchite*), part. of *utsu*, to strike. See *Sori*.
Uye, above. *Mi no uye* (self-of-above), concerning oneself (idiom). Notes, 30 | 5.

W.

Wa, see Aston, § 7. Notes, 2, 11 | 6, 13 | 9, 17 | 2, 3, 23 | 1, 25 | 3, and 27 | 4.
Wadsūka, trifling.
Wadzurai, disease. *Tachi wadzurai*, a standing, a chronic malady. *Tachi*, root of *tatsū*, to stand.

Wadzurai-kurushinde, being ill and in pain. *Kurushinde* (for *kurushimite*), part. of *kurushimu*, to suffer pain.
Waga, one's own. *Waga-de*, single-handed. *De* = *te*, hand, with the nigori. Notes, 22 | 5.
Wakaki, young. Written form of *wakai*. Notes, 31 | 5.
Wakaranū, neg. of *wakaru*, to understand.
Waki, side.
Warai, root of *warau*, to laugh. *Warai-gawo*, smiling countenance. *Gawo* = *kawo*, face, with the nigori.
Ware, I.
Warū (for *waruku*), bad.
Washi (vulg. for *watakūshi*), I. Aston, § 14. Notes, 12 | 4, 31 | 3.
Watakushi, I. Notes, 25 | 3, 27 | 4.
Wo, the particle which is the sign of the accusative case, or *wo kaku*. Aston, § 10 Notes, 28 | 9.

Y.

Ya, or, A dubitative or interrogative particle.
Yado, house, dwelling.
Yaki, root of *yaku*, to roost. *Yaki-mono*, roast, *rôti*.
Yaku, office, use. Notes, 10 | 3.
Yama-dera, mountain-temple. *Dera* = *tera*, temple, with the nigori. Notes, 23 | 9.
Yamimasenū, polite neg. of *yamu*, intrans. verb, to cease.
Yara, an interrogative used when no answer is expected, the inquiry being rhetorical. Notes, 7. *Nani yara shirimasenū*, what it is I know not. Also, 'or.' From *ya*, interrogative and *aran*, old written future form of *aru*, to be. *Dō yara, kō yara*, somehow or other; *lit.*, how will it be? will it be thus?
Yari, root of *yaru*. *Yari wa senū* (I do not the giving), a strong neg. instead of *yaranū* which is the neg. of *yaru*. Notes, 12 | 6, 7. See *Senū*. *Yari-tsukeyō*, will effect. *Tsukeyō*, fut. of *tsuku*, to stick. Notes, 31 | 9.
Yaru, to give.
Yatsū, fellow! in a bad sense. See *Koitsū*.
Yatsū, eight.
Ye, towards.
Ye, an expletive; a particle having no translateable meaning, although it is sometimes not unlike the English, Eh! It is tacked on to phrases, as *sō ka ye*, is it so, indeed! *toreta ka ye*, has it taken itself away? Notes, 11 | 4.
Yei-yō, prosperity, luxury. Notes, 29 | 5.
Yekubo, dimple.
Yemasenū, polite neg. of *yeru*, to get.
Yen, verandah. Notes, 30 | 8.
Yen-ja, family connections.
Yerai, choice (adj.). Notes, 16 | 6.
Yete, part. of *yeru*, to get, to get at, to find out.
Yetoku, to comprehend, comprehension. *Ye*, root of *yeru*, to get; *toku*, to understand. Notes, 19 | 1, 2.
Yo, night.
Yō, function! also matter, business. *Yō ni tatsū*, to be of use.
Yō, kind, sort, fashion. *Yōna*, sort, like; *-na* for *naru*, to be. *Yōni*, in the manner. Notes, 25 | 6, 27 | 9.
Yō (for *yoku*), well.
Yobi-okoshite, part. of *yobi-okosu*, to call up. *Yobi*, root of *yobu*, to call; *okosu*, caus. of *okoru*, to arise.
Yoi, the commencement of evening.
Yoi, good.
Yōi, preparation.
Yō-jin (use-heart) watchfulness, heed. *Jin* is *shin* with the nigori.
Yō-jō (to nourish, life), taking care of oneself. Notes, 18 | 6.
Yokei, more than enough, excessive.
Yokeredo (*yoku-keredo*), although it were good.
Yoki, good. Notes, 20 | 1.
Yoku, well (adv.).
Yomu, to read. *Uta wo yomu*, to compose the Japanese poetry called *uta*. Notes, 24 | 2, 3.
Yōna. See *Yō*.
Yōni. See *Yō*.
Yori, than, from.
Yoroshiki, good. Written form of *yoroshii*. Notes, 20 | 1.
Yoshi, account, purport.

Yoshi, good. *Yoshi-ashi*, good or bad.
Yō-shō (infant-little), young child.
Yoso, elsewhere, others.
Yotsu, four. Notes, 24 | 4.
Yotte (for *yorite*), part. of *yoru*, to approach. Much used in the sense of 'in reference to,' as *to iu koto ni yotte*, in reference to the thing named, Notes, 2; *kore ja ni yotte*, in reference to this being so, therefore.
Yubi, finger. *Oya yubi*, parent finger, thumb; *hito sashi* (man, to point) *yubi*, the index; *taka-daka* (tall-tall) *yubi*, middle finger; *mūmei no yubi, na nashi yubi, beni-sashi yubi*, the nameless, rouge-putting, third finger; *ko yubi*, the little finger. See also *Shi*, the Chinese word for finger.
Yudan, negligence.
Yugami, root of *yugamu*, to be distorted. As a noun, distortion.
Yugande, part. of *yugamu*, to be distorted.
Yū-jo, haunt of dissipation. Notes, 26 | 3.
Yukanū, neg. of *yuku*.
Yukazu, neg. of *yuku*. Notes, 22 | 5.
Yuki, root of *yuku*.
Yukō, fut. of *yuku*.
Yuku (or *iku*) to go. As a noun, 'the going.'
Yururito, leisurely.
Yusan (amusement-mountain), pleasure excursion.
Yuye, because.

Z.

Za, seat.
Zachu (seat-middle), room. *Zachu no hito*, the company. Notes, 25 | 7.
Zazen, the act of sitting in meditation like a Buddhist priest. Notes, 16 | 6.
Zen, previous. **Zemban**, previous evening; *n* becoming *m* before *b*.
Zo, an emphatic particle. Notes, 8 | 6, 12 | 2, 14 | 4. *Nani zo*, emphatically, what!
Zonji, root of *zonzuru*. As a noun, 'knowledge.' *Ji* = *shi*, root of *suru*, with the nigori. Notes, 25 | 8.
Zonji-dashi-mashitareba, when the thought struck me. See *Zonji* and *Dashi*. *Mashitareba*, condit. past of *masū*.
Zonjimasenedo, though I do not know. Neg. concess. of *zonjimasū*.
Zonjimasū, honorif. form of *zonzuru*. *Ji* = *shi*, root of *suru*, with the nigori.
Zonjimasureba, when I think, condit. of *zonjimasū*.
Zonzuru, to think, to know. *Zon*, to think; *zuru* = *suru*, with the nigori.
Zō-sui, a hotch-potch of rice, herbs, and other ingredients.
Zoto, quietly, secretly, stealthily.

KIU-O DO-WA.

NI NO JO.

ERRATA IN THE SERMON.

Page 8, notes, lines 9 and 10, Read,—*riyō tonari* being the neighbours to the right and left, and *mukō sangen* being the three opposite houses.

Page 10, line 5, second *no*, and line 6, second *no*. A reference should have been given to the Vocabulary and to the Notes p. 6, line 1, 2 and p. 29, line 3. The references are to the lines of the Japanese.

Page 10, notes, line 3, for *torite* read *tōrite*.

Page 25, notes, line 9, for *zō* read *zo*.

With regard to the Title printed at each end of the Sermon and at the head of the pages, it should be stated that the use of capital letters alone has prevented it from being printed as it should be,—Kiu-Ō Dō-wa. See also notes to page 1.

わる様に成まする。兎角何事も心のさじや。
ドウゾ儘ならぬ我なさなされぬ様の御用心を
御たのミ申まする　休貞

iru yō ni narimasuru. To-kaku, nani-goto mo kokoro
to live manner in to become what thing soever heart
becomes solely one of tears. In one form or another, all things are matters of

no koto ja. | Dō zo, mina sama o naki nasarenū yō no
matter (de aru) all gentlemen to weep not to do
the heart. I implore all of you to take heed that you do not weep.

go yō-jin wo | o tanomi mōshimasuru. Kiu-sokū.
heed to request to say Rest

(Notes to page 33.)

To-kaku [1], see note to page 27.
Dō zo [2], *lit.*, 'how,' with the particle of great emphasis, *zo*, but without interrogation, *i.e.*, as it were, 'in every manner,' and thence the idiomatic expression means entreating, beseeching, desiring = Please, I pray, I wish.
Mina sama [2] implies the second person.
Dō zo, etc. [2, 3]. The sentence more *lit.* is, Please, all you gentlemen, I say-request heed of the manner not to weep. That is, to avoid the course which he has shown leads to weeping.
Kiu-sokū [3], Pause. Indicates that the sermons will be resumed.

ku wo ukeru no de gozarimasŭ. Hĭto-tabi hon-shin wo
pain to receive (mono) to be once original heart
receiving of all kinds of pain. When once the comprehension

yetokŭ | sureba, naranŭ koto wa naranŭ to shiri, nangi na
to comprehend when one does that to know (naru)
of the original heart is reached, knowing that a wrong thing is wrong, understanding

koto wa | nangi to gaten shĭte, shiite mi wo nogareyō to wa
comprehension doing self
that a woeful thing is a woe, one does not attempt to rescue oneself,

itashi-| masenŭ. Kore wo Chuyō ni wa, "Fū-ki, hin-sen, iteki,
this rich-noble poor-mean barbarian
whether or no. This is called in the Chuyo, "When the superior man ap-

"kwan, nan; | kun-shi iru to shĭte, jitoku sesu to iu koto
calamity difficulty superior man to enter when doing understanding not doing
"pears (iru) the thing called not understanding does not exist, whether the rich and noble,

"nashi" to iute | gozarimasuru. Kono aji ga shiremasenŭ
not to be being said is this taste not to be known
"the poor and mean, the barbarian, calamity, difficulty." If this taste be not known,

to, ku-raku wa karada ni | aru yōni oboyete, kokoro wa waki ye
pain-pleasure body in to be as if feeling heart side towards
feeling as if pain and pleasure are in the body, leaving the heart aside

sŭtete-oite, hĭtasura-| ni katachi no raku wo motomuru tokoro
leaving alone earnest - ly appearance comfort to seek circumstance
in consequence of (kara) earnestly seeking the comfort of the exterior;

kara; ogori ni utsuri, rin-shoku | ni nari, kayette kokoro ni ku
prodigality to pass parsimonious to become contrariwise pain
passing into prodigality (or) becoming parsimonious, obtaining contrariwise pain

wo ukete, naite bakari |
receiving weeping
in the heart, their existence

(Notes to page 32.)

Naranŭ koto [2], see page 31.
Surebe [2] is impersonal here. See remarks page 19 as to *nasaremasurŭ* and *go yetokŭ*.
Shiite [3], see page 27, and vocabulary. *Shiite*, etc., *i.e.* more *lit.* 'Whether or no thinking that he will rescue himself he does not.' *Omōte*, or perhaps *shĭte*, is understood after *to*. *Nagareyō* is the future. See remarks under *arō* and *gozarimashō*, in the vocabulary and notes, as to the conditional signification of the future.
Chu-yō (4), the second book of Confucius.
Fū-ki, etc. [4], *i.e.*, the superior man is never at a loss how to conduct himself in the most varied circumstances.
Tokoro [8], see notes pp. 16, 18.
Ogori ni, etc. [8], *i.e*, they fall into extravagant extremes.
Kayette [9], *i.e.* contrariwise to their search for *katachi no rakŭ*, they obtain *kokoro ni ku*.
Naite, etc. [9], more *lit.*, 'they become into the way of living, weeping only.'

苦(く)とうけるのでござります。一(ひと)たび本心(ほんしん)を會得(ゑとく)
すまいぞ。ならぬ事はならぬと知(し)て難儀(なんぎ)な事(こと)は
なんぎと合点(がてん)しく。強(しひ)て死(し)を遁(のが)れまうとはいたし
ませぬ。是を中庸(ちうよう)には富貴(ふうき)貧賤(ひんせん)夷狄(いてき)患難(くわんなん)
君子(くんし)入(いる)として自得(じとく)せずといふ事(こと)なしといふて
ござります。此味(このあぢはひ)がしれませぬと苦楽(くらく)は動(うごく)に
なるやうに恐(おそれ)て。心(こころ)をわすれ捨(すて)置(おい)て。ひきずら
れ眼(うちち)の楽(らく)をもとむるところから奢(おごり)にうつり安樂(あんらく)
となり。却(かへつ)てこゝろに苦(く)をうけて泣(なく)てござり

かり。是がござらじや。そこにかかりなしう。うぎさわきに
うろ鳴ぬぞといふが。麻がぬりしね鳥しく。イエく
わしいかまへ岩のなくれを次に春きのでござると
いつて。ナント おりしろへ味ぐござりますが。老ぬ
ともきも男も女も。命の有も金乃なくも。
おかしなろしく。昼夜慈歎乃いゑいやてきませぬ。
ちまきが夢心の物ひじや。平青なしてござりの
此ひつき此傷手のしかふ。たましめ事を心理
やろふをりまつてするを分別らう。さるぐの

iru. "Kore wa dō ja? Soko ni iru nara, naze sakki ni | kara
to be this how (de aru) there to remain why before in from
"How is this? If you are remaining there, why do you not cry ere

"nakanŭ zo?" to iyeba, shika ga nukaranŭ kawo de:— "Iye, iye, |
not to cry when he said deer unconscious face with
"this?" thus when he said, the deer, with an innocent face said:— "No, no,

"washi wa omaye-gata no naku no wo kiki ni kita no de
I you (plural) to cry (mono) to hear come (mono)
"*I* came to hear *your* lamentations."

"gozaru" to | iuta.
to be said.

Nanto! omoshiroi hanashi de gozarimashō ga, oitaru | mo
amusing story will be both
What do you say! is it not an amusing story? but both old and

wakaki mo, otoko mo onna mo, kane no aru mo kane no nai
and men women money to have not to have
young, men and women, rich and poor,

mo, | oshi-narashite chu-ya shiutan no koye wa yamimasenŭ. | Kore
day-night lamentation voice not to cease this
all together, day and night, the voice of lamentation ceases not. This

ga mina kokoro no wadsurai ja. Hikkiyō, sŭkoshi bakari no |
all heart disease (de aru) a little only
is all a disease of the heart. In fine, on account of only a little

mibiiki migatte no tame ni naranŭ koto wo muri-| yari ni yari-
selfishness egotism account on not to become thing
selfishness and egotism they do (the) effecting recklessly of what is wrong:

tsukeyō to suru: mufumbetsŭ kara sama-zama no |
to do want of judgment from all kinds
from want of judgment there is a

(Notes to page 31.)

Nara [1], for *nareba*, if (you) be. **Nukaranŭ** [2]. See vocabulary.

Washi [3], familiar style; so is *omaye-gata*. The more *lit.* translation is, As to me, I am a come-thing to hear the cry-things of you.

Gozarimashō [4]. The future here implicates a doubt, and thus, in asking a question to which no reply is required, there is no interrogative particle *ka* to finish the sentence. The *ga* may be translated, 'but.'

Oitaru [4], for *oi to aru* (not *te aru*), he who is old.

Wakaki [5] written form for *wakai*.

Oshi-narashite [6] *lit.* to thrust-striking an average. ? all together.

Naranŭ koto [8], a wrong thing; 'unbecoming thing' is literal and almost accurate.

Sama [9], appearance, manner; *sama-zama*, all manner.

Muri-yari ni [9], un(*mu*)reasonable-to do-ly = recklessly.

Yari-tsukeyō [9], to do-will fix = will effect.

"**aisatsŭ sureba, niyobō no hiiki wo suru to, haha-oya no kigen**
mediation when I do wife mother-parent feelings
"when I try to make peace, if I take my wife's part, (my) mother's feelings are

"**ga | sokonemasuru. Niyobō wo shikareba, 'ta-nin ja to omōte, |**
to hurt if I scold stranger (de aru) considering
"hurt. If I scold my wife, (saying) considering (me) as

"**'hitori mugō-tsurō sassharu' to urami. Iya, mō naka**
cruel hard to treat already middle
"'a stranger, you treat a lone woman cruelly and hardly,' she detests (me). Alas! having be-

"**ni | tatta hashira de, tsurai no kurushii no to mōsŭ yōna koto**
set up post hard ~~(sono)~~ or painful to call sort of affair
"come a post set up between them, it is not the sort of matter to be called hard or

"**de wa | gozarimasenŭ" to, hiyōshi ni kakatte mi no uye no**
is not harmony in self
"painful" thus (saying) in chorus twaddling on about their personal

nangi-| banashi;
trouble to talk
troubles;

Sono uchi ni, hitori, ki ga tsuite:—"Hon ni mō shika ga |
a man mind applying truth in already deer
Meanwhile one of them bethinking himself:— "In truth the deer ought to bell

"**nakisōna mono ja. Amari hanashi ni shikori ga kite, shika**
cry-like (de aru) to much talk engrossment by coming
"by this time. Having come to be engrossed by too much talk, I do

"**no | ne wo kiki-hadsŭshita ka shiranŭ" to, yen no**
cry to hear missed not to know verandah
"not know whether we have missed hearing the cry of the deer," thus (saying) drawing back

shōji wo hiki-| akete mireba, ōkina shika ga niwa-saki ni
to draw opening when he looked great garden front
the slides of the verandah, when he looked (out), a great deer was standing silently in

mokunen to shite |
silently doing
the front of the garden

(Notes to page 29 continued.)

smoke, as a ceiling; means also, idiomatically, to be unhappy. *Kŭsŭbutte imasŭ* = I am wretched. **Isso** [8]. Or ? 'once for all,' 'for good and all;' or perhaps for *itsu zo*, some time or other. **Sato** [9], village, is used for the wife's home or family. *Sato ye kayesuru*, is to send (the wife) back to (her) family,—to divorce her. *Kayesuru*, caus. of *kayeru*. He would divorce his wife only that he has two little children.

(Notes to page 30.)

Aisatsŭ-nin is a peace-maker, a mediator. **Hiiki** [1], partiality, favoritism. *Hiiki wo sŭru*, to favour. **Hitori** [3]. *Hitori-mono* is a person without relations; *hitori-mi* is solitary, without kindred. We here translate *hitori*, when used by the complaining wife, as 'lone woman.' **To** [3, 5 and 8]. *Iute*, saying, is understood. **De** [4]. *Atte*, being, is understood. **Tsurai** [4]. Just our common expression, 'Hard is no name for it.' The saying about the post probably refers to some familiar proverb. **Kakatte** [5], *lit.*, 'being connected with,' but *koye wo kakeru* is to lift up the voice, and *ki ni kakeru*, to brood over. *Kakatte* is the part. of *kakaru*, to be hung up; *kakeru* is 'to hang up.' **Mi no uye** [5]. *Uye* is 'above,' but the phrase is idiomatic, meaning, 'concerning oneself.' **Sono uchi ni** [6] More *lit.* 'in the inside of that' (which precedes), meanwhile. **Yen** [8]. The *y* is silent. **Shōji** [8]. Slides formed of paper pasted on wooden frames.

挨拶すれバ女房の贔屓をすると。母親の機嫌が
そこねますの。女房を叱れバ。他人じやと思つて
ひがむゆゑ。ほんにどうしやうもなく憂く。イヤモウ中々
ふたつ様ぐ。ほんに心の苦しいのやらかやうする事でる
ござりませぬと。物好にかゝつて。身のうへ此難儀
ござりまし。其内に一人気が狂て。ほんにモウ癪が
嘆きますのじや。あまり心労に苦りが募く。癪の
事を案じまうじてぬと。縁の障子を引
あけてみますれば。大きな癪が庭さきに。懸命して

験担でござれども。又親類縁者じやのう。今の
ふびんをつまらする。勘定としてもまといはれまする。
家内つましのかりの人。ごともまさつまりまするので
ござりまするとも随分つとまらず。隣の人がナエく
いづれも猶のことも栄耀じや。私の渡りますを
けいまくなされてやさりませ。どうしても果て家
内のものと。母との中がわるうござりて。日うす一日
牛の角つき合。内中がもてばうりまする。男イツソ
里へ帰りませうと思へど。幼少のまれれ新人も有

"-tan go mottomo de gozaredomo, mata shinrui yenja domo
still relations connections (plural)
" for the lamentations of all of you, still, money being continually begged

"kara kane no | mushin wo iwaretari, 'Ingiyō wo shite-kure' to
from money seal doing
" from relations and connections, 'Please put your seal' being

"iwaretari; | kanaidzure no kakari-udo, kore mo mata komatta
too likewise vexing
" continually said, poor relations, these too are vexing matters

"mono de | gozarimasuru" to hambun iwasasu, tonari no hito
half neighbour
" likewise" thus not allowing him half to speak, a neighbouring man

ga:— "Iye, iye, | idzure mo sama no wa, mina yeiyō ja.
all gentlemen all prosperity
(says):— "No, no, as to the (affairs) of all you gentlemen, all is prosperity.

"Watakŭshi no tsurai koto wo | o kiki nasarete kudasarimase.
I hard matter to hear being pleased deign
" Be so kind as to listen to my hard lines.

"Dō shĭta koto yara, ka-|nai no mono to haha to no naka ga
how done affair will be mother
" I know not how it occurs, the relations of (my) wife and mother being bad,

"warŭ gozatte, higana-ichi-nichi | ushi no tsuno dzuki-ai uchi-ju ga
being the whole day cow horn to butt each other
" butting at each other with cows' horns all day long, when, because

"kŭsŭborimasŭ yuye, isso | sato ye kayeshimashō to omoyeba, yō-shō
because resolutely when I think youth
" my home is (thus) made miserable, I resolutely think about divorcing, there

"no mono wa futari mo ari; |
persons two even to be
" are two little children;

(Notes to page 29.)

Mottomo [1], adv.; 'right,' 'most,' 'in the highest degree'; has an idiomatic force. *Go mottomo de gozarimasŭ*, you are certainly right. **Mushin** [2], *lit.*, not-heart. The Japanese is *kokoro nashi*. A reluctant request, a reluctant begging. **Kure** [2], imperative of *kureru;* see *kurete*, page 28. **Ingiyō**, etc. [2]. As is said in English, 'Give me your name,' or 'Back this bill for me.' **Kanaidzure**, etc. [3], 'family-to accompany.' The *no* must often, as here, be rendered by the verb 'to be.' *Kakari-udo* is the same as *kakari-bito*, a man who is connected, a hanger-on. It is the established term for poor relations. The phrase is *lit.* 'the family company who are hangers on.' See first note, page 6. **Iwasasu** [4], neg. of caus. of *iu*, to say. Governs *rōjin*, page 28, line 9. **Yeiyō** [5]. The *i* is not in the hiragana text, but is generally in the dictionaries. **Idzure**, etc. [5]. *Mono*, affair, is understood after *no*. **Kanai no mono** [6, 7], one of the many terms for 'wife.' *Lit.*, person of the family. *Go kanai sama* is 'your wife'; *naigi* (*nai* = private, domestic) is used only of another's wife. *O kami san*, your wife; used also in addressing a married woman = Mrs. *Kami* is superior; *san*, a contraction of *sama* = Mr. *Oku sama* (*oku*, 'innermost,' as *kokoro no oku*, the inmost recesses of the heart), *sai*, *sai-jo* (*jo* = woman), and *niyō-bō* (woman-chamber) are other terms. *Nai-hō* (domestic side, *uchi kata*) and *tsŭma* are obsolete. **Naka** [7], middle, inside, between; comes idiomatically to mean the state of feeling or relations between persons; thus, *naka ga warui*, is our 'on bad terms.' *Naka ga yoi* is said of friends; *noita* (past tense of *noku*, to depart from) *naka*, estranged terms, the relation that exists between strangers. **Uchi-ju** [8], (house-inside), *ju* = *chu* with nigori. Translated 'my home.' **Kŭsuboru** [8], to be blackened by [smoke

"jibun hiki-oi wo koshirayete-kurete wa, shu-jin wa nani ni |
when debt making master what into
"incurring debts, what is to become of the

"narimasuru mono ja? Sore kara mireba, anata no wa | waga
to become thing (de aru) that from if one looks you of one's own
"master? Looking from my point of view, yours is only a case of

"ko ni kane wo tsukawareru bakari no koto" to iyeba, mata |
child by money to be spent only thing again
"money being spent by one's own child," thus when he said, again

katawara kara, "Iya! iya! mise no shu ni kane wo tsukawareru
side shop people
from beside him, "No! no! money being spent by the people of the shop is a

wa mada-[shimo ja; kochi domo wa chikagoro tsūgō ga warū
yet low I (plural) lately circumstance bad
"small matter; as to us, things turning out badly of late,

"gozatte, | tokui-saki ga kata-hashi kara taoremasuru, achira de wa
being customers that
"the customers one after the other become bankrupt, on that side three

"san | gwamme, kochira de wa go kwamme, jitsu ni ki no heru
3 this 5 really mind to decrease
"kwamme, on this side five kwamme, really it is so that one loses

"yō ni | gozarimasū" to iu shīta kara, mukō no seki ni suwatte
fashion to be opposite seat squatting
"heart" thus, so soon as (one) speaks, an old man who was squatting

iru | rōjin ga ōgi wo pachi-pachi narashi nagara:—"Idzure mo no
to remain old man fan whilst
opposite, whilst fiddling with (his) fan :— "Although there is

"go ariu- |
lamen-
"good reason

(Notes to page 28.)

Kurete [1]. Participle of *kureru*, an honorific auxiliary, like *kudasareru*.
Shu-jin, etc. [1], *lit.*, 'as to the master, he is a thing to become what?'
Mata, etc. [3, 4], *i.e.*, another begins to speak, saying, "*Iya, iya,*" etc. *Mata katawara kara* [3, 4]......... *to iu shīta kara* [8]. Again, from beside him ....so soon as (one) speaks, thus,—
Kata-hashi kara [6], *lit.*, 'half-end from,' *i.e.*, from one end towards the other.
Taoremasuru [6]. See vocabulary.
Achira de wa, etc. [6, 7]. That is, by one he loses three, by another five kwamme, and so on. The first *kwamme* takes the nigori for euphony. I am not quite clear as to the value of the kwamme here.
To iu shīta kara [8], *lit.*, 'from below his saying,' *i.e.*, 'after he said.' This adverbial phrase has a very close meaning in point of time = immediately after.
Rōjin [9]. See note to *iwasazu*, page 29.
Wo [9] has been omitted from the Japanese text by an *erratum*. The sentence more *lit.* is, Whilst causing his fan to sound *pachi-pachi*.

ゆへ引負をこしらへて逃亡する。主人も家業
成まするものじや。それゆへ見まする。なにごとのも
我子に金を渡しまするづりのあてとなる。まづ
うろたへるから。イヤく店の店に金を渡しまするは猶ぞ
しることじや。此方どもへ其帳合がよろしうござりて。
ゆゑさきざきがかくさうから例を出まする。つらつてへこ
貴用。これらでへ又申用実に気の減る中より
ござりまする。ひとへ下ゆる。自人の席にまゐらしく存。
老人が扇ぜらくなりしあがら。ゆゑまゐるの御慈

はへく出されしると。袖うら四十又六十男がイやく
なうまこのよな難儀といやその畢竟御子息に
なる今持つてとつきの事く。後く心配する
ござりますゆへ。それなどい中くた様な事でも
ござりませぬ。兎角三年店のものども。売物
までも引負をいたして。又拾両へまして。七拾両を
使ました。年くの帳面の明キ。よつかげめしまく
ござりません。息子の時分う世話をいたし
て。ござりうかかくやらおしげばかり店の用に

tsuite hanasareru to, soba kara shi ju go roku na otoko ga,
drawing to speak when beside from 4 10 5 6 (aaru) man
he spoke drawing sighs, from beside (him) a man of 45 or 46, (says)

"**Iya, iya, | anata no wa, go nangi to wa mōsu mono no hikkiyō**
you trouble to call thing after all
" Excuse me, as to your case, the thing called your troubles being, after all, an

"**go shisoku ni | kane tsukawaruru to iu made no koto de, shiite**
son by money to be spent so much as affair
" affair of so much as to say money being spent by your son, it will

"**go shimpai ni mo | gozarimasŭmai. Watakŭshi nado wa naka-**
anxiety even will not be tho-
" not be urgent cause for anxiety. As to such as I it is

"**naka sayōna koto de wa | gozarimasenŭ. Tokaku kin-nen mise**
roughly such of late years shop
" a thoroughly different matter. Somehow or other of late

"**no mono domo ga karisome | ni mo hiki-oi wo itashite, go ju**
people (plural) trifle in even debt making 5 10
" years (the) people of (my) shop, getting into debt even for trifles, think-

"**riyō wa mamayo, shichi ju riyō wa | mamayo to, nen-nen no**
7 10 yearly
" ing that fifty riyos are nothing, that seventy riyos are nothing, year by year

"**chō-men no aki, yō oboshimeshite | gorōjimase. Hana tare no**
ledger empty nose to drip
" the ledger is emptier, well reflecting please to look. Having taken

"**jibun kara, sewa wo itashi-| te, dō yara kō yara sŭkoshi bakari**
period from trouble doing a little only
" trouble (with them) since the nose-dripping time, after all, when they come to be of some

"**mise no yō ni tatsu |**
" little use in the shop

(Notes to page 27.)

Hanasareru [1] is the potential or passive. **Iya, iya** [1]. An exclamation of dissent. **Anata no** [2]. *Mono*, translated 'case,' is understood. **Go shisokŭ** [2]. The honorific shews that another person is addressed, and supplies the place of a pronoun of the second person. **Koto de** [3]. *Aite*, being, is understood. **Shiite** [3], the part. of *shiiru*, to urge, etc., used adverbially. *Shiite sake wo nomu*, to force oneself to drink sake; more *lit.*, urging, to drink. The sentence in the text is more *lit.*, 'urging, it will not be even (your) 'anxiety.' **Watakushi nado wa** [4], *lit.*, 'as to me, et cætera,' but resembles the French phrase, *nous autres*, or the vulgar phrase 'the likes of me.' **Naka-naka**, etc., [4], *lit.*, 'thoroughly, as to such an affair being, it is not.' *Aite*, being, is, as usual, understood after *de*. **Tokaku** [5 and p. 33, 1]. The Chinese characters used for this word are merely phonetic and not ideographic. *To*, outside = 'that,' and *kaku*, 'this manner.' It has the meanings, 'in that way and this way,' 'in various ways,' 'in one way and another,' etc. **Domo** [5], a humble form of the plural. **Riyō** [6], a unit of money, not a coin. **Mamayo** [6, 7]. An adverbial exclamation, 'no matter,' 'never mind!' **To** [7]. *Omōte*, thinking, is understood. **Dō yara**, etc. [9], *lit.*, 'how will it be, will it be thus!' = 'somehow or other.' Here translated, 'after all.' **Yō ni tatsŭ jibun** [9], *lit.*, 'to stand to use period.'

"**komatta yatsŭ de, watakŭshi ga yado ni 'imasureba, shiburа-**
troublesome rascal I house when I am lazi-
being a troublesome rascal, when I am at home,

"**kobura | to mise no yō wo te-tsŭtaimasuredo, watakŭshi no kage**
ly shop business although he lends a hand shadow
although he lends a hand lazily to the business of the shop, when my shadow is not

"**ga miye-|nŭ to, shiri ni ho kake de yŭ-jo gayoi. Mochiron**
not to be seen when back sail to hang up certainly
"seen, hoisting a sail on his back, he is off to some haunt. Although

"**shinrui yenja | domo mo iro-iro to kiyōkun wo itashite kure-**
relations connections (plural) in various ways instruction doing altho'
" (his) relations and connections kindly give him instruction in various ways,

"**masuredo, | ikkō ŭma no mimi ni kase dō yō. Ano yōna**
they give wholly horse ear wind same manner that like
" (it is) wholly the same as wind in a horse's ear. When I think

"**yatsŭ ni shindai wo | makasaniya naranŭ ka to sonjimasureba,**
rascal property when I think
"of the possibility of having to entrust (my) property to a rascal like that,

"**kokoro-bosoi | mono de gosarimasŭ. O kage de, nani hitotsŭ**
sad one thing
" it is a sad affair. I feel thankful that my condition

"**fŭsokŭ no nai | watakŭshi no mibun naredomo, ko yuye ni mai**
deficient I condition son because of every
" is not wanting (in) any one thing, but nevertheless, because of (my) son,

"**nichi mai yo chi no | namida——. Saritote wa, komatta mono**
day night blood tears painful
" every day (and) every night, tears of blood——. This being so, it is a painful thing"

"**ja" to, toiki wo |**
(de aru) thus sighs
thus (saying) when .

(Notes to page 26.)

De [1] *Atte*, being, is understood. **Ga** [1] is here the genitive particle. See *Aston's Written Grammar*, p. 45. **To** [2] *Shite*, doing, is understood. **Kage ga miyenŭ** [2] *i.e.*, as soon as my back is turned. **Gayoi** [3] *Kayoi*, root of *kayō*, to resort, to frequent. *Yŭ-jo*, a place of amusement. *Suru*, to do, is understood after *gayoi*, where the sentence breaks off effectively. **Makasaniya naranŭ** [6] *lit.*, If I do not entrust, it does not become; a very common idiom, meaning, I must entrust. With the interrogative *ka*, the meaning is, 'must I not entrust?'. The more *lit.* translation of the whole phrase is, 'To a rascal like that, must I not entrust property !—thus (*to*) when I think,' &c. **O kage de** [7], *lit.*, by honorable help, I feel thankful. *Kage* is shadow, and thence, influence, help. See p. 25. **Nani** [7], what; translated here, 'any.' **Naredomo** [8]. Altho' it is. *-Domo* is separated in the translation, and expressed by 'but nevertheless.' **Chi no namida** [8, 9]. Another sentence broken off without a verb, for effect. **Komatta mono ja** [9], *i.e.*, my heart is broken. **To** [9]. *Iute*, saying, is understood.

こ御ざる奴じや。私が宿に居ますれば。ちづつてぶらぶら
と居の用をも手傳ひ申ますぞ。私のうけがよく
ぬく。氣に懸りまして拙者がまゝ。勿論親類縁者
どもゝ。いろいろと意見をいたして呉ますれども。
一向馬乃耳に風同様。アノやうなやつが身代を
ゆづりますると存じますれども心細い
ものでござります。おらげ何一ツ不足の事
私の身分なれども。子故に毎日毎夜血の
なみだ。さりとてものじやと。吐息を

男気をおこして。さて今晩はいづれもさまの
おかげで。酔ながら男とお相がゝりをいたして酔は
たのしみをいたし申さ。ありがたう私しか扱て
案しんて居ますれど。さてめでたく家内のものが
心づかひをいたして居ませうと。ふ肖ぞんじ出し
申しますぞ。どうやら酒が手へいるやうに覚へく
ますといふ。座中の人々。其まゝどうぞいたし続く
ござり申すぞサア。御大きくござりませ。御ぞんじの通り
主人の粋当年廿二歳に成まするが。さうとてへ

otoko sakadsuki wo maye ni hikayete, "Sate, komban wa idsure
man wine cup before stopping now to-night on all-
fifty stopping the wine-cup in front of him, says "Now, with the assistance of all you

"mo sama no | o kage de yoi kara yururito o monogatari wo
sides gentlemen with at one's ease stories
gentlemen since the commencement of the evening, telling stories

"itashite, yoi | tanoshimi wo itashimashita. Shikashi nagara, wata-
doing good pleasure we have done however
at our ease, we have had good pleasure. However, when

"-kushi wa kayōni | tanoshinde orimasuredo, sadamete kanai
thus being joyful tho' I am doubtless
"the thought suddenly struck me that (to) although I am thus joyful, doubtless my family

"no mono ga | kokoro-dsukai wo itashite imashō to futo sonji-
anxiety doing may be suddenly
"may be in a state of anxiety,

"dashi- | mashitareba, dō yara sake ga ri ni iru yō ni oboye-|masu"
(see vocab.) (vocab.) to enter to feel
"somehow or other I feel as if the wine was disagreeing with

to iu. Zachu no hito ga, "Sore wa dō itashita wake de |
to say that how made reason
"me." One of the company (says), "Why is that?"

"gozarimasu so?" "Saa, o kiki kudasarimase. Go sonji no
to listen do (honorific) to know
"Well, be so good as to listen. As you are

tōri, | hitori no segare tō nen ni ju ni sai ni narimasuru ga,
manner one man this year 2 10 2 to become
"aware, my only youngster becomes twenty-two years (of age) this year, but,

"saritote wa, |
"nevertheless,

(Notes to page 24 continued.)

called One, Two or Three, and as the other numbers run the reverse way from ours, the following is the singular result:—

Japanese	Nine	English	midnight (or noon).
,,	Eight	,,	Two
,,	Seven	,,	Four
,,	Six	,,	Six
,,	Five	,,	Eight
,,	Four	,,	Ten
,,	Nine (again)	,,	Noon (or midnight.)

Issai [6], *lit.*, 'one cut,' *i.e.*, 'a trifling portion.' When joined to a negative, as here, it means 'in no way'; giving, with a change of words, the same meaning as *tonto* in the preceding sentence. **Naki-sōna mono** [6, 7], *lit.*, a 'to-cry-like thing.' **Uchi ni** [9], *lit.*, 'in the inside' (of their being silent), *i.e.*, while.

(Notes to page 25.)

'Says' [1] is the *iu* of line 7. **Kage** [2], *lit.*, shadow, has come to mean 'protection,' 'help.' See p. 26. **Watakushi wa** [3], 'as to me,' 'for my part.' **Kanai no mono** [4], *ka*, house; *nai*, inside; *mono*, persons; the persons of my house, my family. **Ri ni iru**, etc. [6], *lit.*, I feel as if the wine entered the *ri*. This sentence is somewhat of a difficulty, but the interlinear translation is offered. *Ri* being one's 'inside,' it would appear to mean that the wine affects his 'inside,' affects him deeply, more than it otherwise would; or it may be a Yedo expression, the sermon being in the Yedo dialect, for *avoir le vin mauvais*. **Yō ni** [6], 'in the manner;' translated, 'as if.' **Zachu** [7], seat-middle. The persons in a room, the company. **Sore wa**, etc. [7], *lit.*, as to that, on account of *(de)* a how-made reason is it? *Zo* is an emphatic particle. **Saa** [8], an interjection. **Go sonji**, etc. [8], more *lit.*, 'manner of honorable knowledge.' **Segare** [9] Son. Humble term, in speaking of one's own son to others. **Sai** [9] Year (of age). *Iku sai*, How old? **Saritote** *(sa ari to iute)*, 'saying that it is thus.'

Kore wo kokoro-ate ni tadzune-yuki, kiyakŭ-den wo kari-uke, |
this (priest) relying to visit to go guest room to hire to receive
Relying on him they went to pay a visit, to engage the guest-room,

tomari - gake no yusan.
to stay all night-to set about excursion.
the excursion was a stay-all-night one.

Shika no ne wo machi-wabite, uta wo | **yomu hito mo ari,**
deer belling to wait suffering poetry persons to be
Being tired waiting for the belling of the deer, some persons compose poetry,

achira de wa shi wo tsŭkuri, kochira de wa hok-|**ku, saitsŭ**
there to make here
there they make Chinese poetry, here they make hokku, passing

osayetsŭ. Iri-ai no koro ni natte mo tonto shika ga | **naki-**
twilight time having become even at all do-
the wine-cup. Even when it became the time of twilight, the deer do not bell (cry) at

masenŭ. Shōya ni natte mo, yotsŭ ni natte mo
not bell beginning night four
all. Even when it became the early part of the night, even when it became ten

shika no | **ne wa issai kikoyesu, "Kore wa dō ja? mō**
not to hear this how already
o'clock, the cry of the deer not being in the least audible, "How is this? the deer

"shika ga naki-|**sōna mono ja" to, matedomo nakasu. Soro-soro**
to cry like thing altho' they wait to cry not gradually
"ought to cry by this time" (so thinking) although they wait, they cry not. Gradually

nebuke wa | **saite-kuru; shi mo uta mo iya ni nari,**
sleepiness opening to come both and to become
sleepiness comes on; both Japanese and Chinese poetry become distasteful things,

akubi ni uki-yo-|**banashi mo togire, mina mokunen to shite iru**
yawningly gossip to suspend all silently doing to be
yawningly they suspend (their) gossip also, while all are silent,

uchi ni, go ju bakari no |
while 5 10 about
a man of about

(Notes to page 24.)

Uta wo yomu [2, 3]. *Yomu* is *lit.*, to read, but the phrase means to compose that sort of Japanese poetry called *uta*, see p. 9. **Achira** [3], 'there,' is the adverb of the third person; *kochira*, 'here,' is that of the first person, and *sochira*, 'there,' that of the second person. **Shi** [3] Chinese poetry. **Hokku** [3, 4]. A shorter kind of verse than the *uta*. The line divides the *kana* thus, *hotsu*|*ku*. **Saitsŭ osayetsŭ** [4]. Passing the wine-cup. The European custom of 'taking wine' with your fellow-guests appears in another form in Japan. There, one drinks first oneself and then passes one's own cup to the person with whom one takes wine. To superiors and guests belongs the giving of the glass, *saitsŭ*. *Osayetsŭ* is the receiving of the glass or cup. **Tonto** [4] has a negative meaning and is used with a negative verb. **Yotsu** [5] *doki*, (*i.e.*, *toki* with the nigori) time, understood. The Japanese four, and the English ten o'clock. The Japanese hour is equal to two English hours. Twice in the day, at six in the morning and afternoon, the English and Japanese numbers for the hour coincide, but as there are no Japanese hours

あまりとんと不辛抱ゆゑ。客殿をうりはらけ。
とりまりげの拒山。麻の葉をゆらりまびく。鈴を
よむ人もありがうちでも侍を作り。こちらでは段
句。さて川押へた。入相のようになつても。トント麻が
なくてませぬ。初夜になつても暁になりても麻の
音して一切眠られしぞ。こまりきつてどうしや。モウ麻がなくて
さうなものじやと。ゆゑでもならずそろそろ眠気ハ
さして来る。侍を鈴もいやになり。おくびまじり夜
惜もとぶれし。ころ陸然としてゐる中に夜中の

とくと行つてる白状をいたしまするがさり迄ゝ
こまつたものじや。是じやに依て何とぞ一念発
心の正根を見失え。人欲の悪根を見捨ずね
なりませぬ。どうぞ此世に一生の道をとりまして
ございます。あまりに付て二つめしろへ暇しが
なる。序に安く下さりませ。秋も夜さむになり
帰られお気に入つてを町人衆が又云人会て
麻の着をきて木曽ぢと何が弁当小竹筒を
用意をし。ある山寺に心やすい和尚があれ。

wo hĭto ni ōte wa hakujō wo itashimasuru. Sari to te wa, |
people meeting to confess he does
his mental distortion. This being so,

komatta mono ja. Kore ja ni yotte, nani to so, ichido hon-|
painful (de aru) In regard to this being so by all means once original
it is a painful case. By all means, therefore, I would that

shin no shōgin wo mi-oboye, jinyoku no akugin wo mi-son-
heart genuine money to see remember man-greed bad money to see-mis-
you and I should not depart from the path all our lives, so that (yō) we should once for all

senŭ | yō dōzo o tagai ni isshō michi ni hanarenŭ yō ni itashĭ-|
take-not fashion mutually life-long path not to stray from would wish
(ichido) see-remember the original heart which is the good money and not see-mistake

tō gozarimasŭ.
to do
greed which is the bad money.

Kore ni tsuite, omoshiroi hanashi ga | aru. Tsuide ni
this sticking amusing story is in the course
In connection with this, there is an amusing story. Be so good

kiite kudasarimase. Aki mo yo-samu ni nari-| mashĭta koro,
hearing be so good autumn already night-cold became time
as to listen. In autumn when the nights had already become cold,

sō-ō ni kurasŭ chōnin shu ga go roku nin ii-awasete | shĭka
suitable-ly to live merchant (plural) 5 6 men to speak-causing to meet deer
five or six well-to-do merchants having consulted together, (thinking) they will go in order

no ne wo kiki ni yukō to, nani ga bentō sasaye wo | yōi
belling to hear will go (see notes) pic-nic box wine flask preparation
to hear the belling of the deer, having got ready the pic-nic box and wine-

wo shi, aru yamadera ni kokoro-yasui oshō ga aru. |
to do to exist mountain-temple intimate priest to be
flask, there was a friendly priest (who lived) in a certain mountain-temple.

(Notes to page 23.)

Wa [1] the force of this particle is well instanced here; as to, in the case of, meeting people.

Hakujō wo itashimasuru [1] *lit.*, he makes disclosure, *i.e.*, he involuntarily betrays his condition.

Hanashi [5] root of *hanasu*, to speak, taken as a noun.

Narimashĭta koro [6, 7]; *lit.*, the became-time, *i.e.*, when it had become.

Sō-ō ni kurasu [7], suitably to live, well-to-do.

Kiki (root) **ni** [8], in order to hear; *kiku* (infin. or pres.) *ni*, in the hearing, whilst hearing.

To [8], *omōte*, thinking, must be supplied here, *vide* Vocabulary under *To*.

Nani ga [8], a detached, filling-up phrase, like the 'and so' of the story-tellers of our youth; *lit.*, something.

Aru yamadera [9], an existing, *i.e.*, a certain mountain temple. *-dera* is *tera* with the nigori in composition.

mono de wa gozarimasenū. Shikashi mata, honshin ni tōzakari,|
original heart
is utterly inadmissible. But again, if one falls away from and

honshin wo mi-wasureru to, izen no tōri makkuro ni natte, |
to see to forget if former like very black having become
forgets the original heart, having become quite black as formerly,

akugin ga miye-nikū narimasuru. Go yō-jin wo nasare-|mase.
bad money to see difficult becomes watchfulness
the bad money becomes difficult to be distinguished. I beg you to be watchful.

Warū suru to, honshin ja yara akushin ja | yara, ware to
bad to do if (de aru) will it be bad heart by oneself
If one acts badly, whether it be the original heart, or a bad heart, by oneself

waga-de ni gaten ga yukasu. Sono kurai | kokoro kara omoi-
one's own hand comprehension not to go this dark heart from to re-
singlehandedly one cannot understand. Because of this benighted heart, if what-

tsūku hodo no koto ga omou yō ni yukanū | to, "haa, sū; haa,
solve on amount to desire fashion not to go (interjections)
ever he intends does not go as he desires, he is obliged, saying

sū" to, kata-de-iki wo seniya naranū. Nangi | na mono ja.
shoulder breath if one do not not to become painful (de aru)
hā! and sū! to sigh. It is a painful matter.

Semete damatte nado ireba yokeredo, | karisome ni mo,
at least being silent &c. if he should remain altho' it were good trifle even
Although it would be better if at least he should remain silent or so, even in trifles,

"kurushii, setsunai" to, hara no uchi no yugami |
distressed uneasy belly inside twisting
saying that he is distressed and uneasy, in case he meets people he betrays

---

(Notes to page 22.)

Tōzakari [1], to become distant from, to be estranged.
Miye-nikū [3], to see-difficult, hard to be distinguished. *Mi-nikū* is ugly.
Waga-de [5], *de* is *te*, hand, with the nigori.
Gaten ga yukasu [5], comprehension does not go. Similar to the idiom in French; *ça ira, Comment ça va!* &c.
Omoi-tsūku hodo no koto [6], the thing amounting to one's intentions.
Seniya (for *seneba*) **naranū** [7] if one does not do so, it does not become. A very common idiom, meaning, one must do so.
To [9] *Iute*, saying, is perhaps to be understood. The meaning then is that he betrays the depravity of his mind to every one he meets, by complaining of being distressed and uneasy even on the smallest occasion.
Hara no uchi, &c. [9]. The Japanese place the mental seat in the stomach. *Lit.*, the twisting of the inside of the belly; internal crookedness; mental distortion.

物でもござりませぬ。ちつと又本心に違ざりつ
私心を見つけまするといゝ。以前の通り真黒になりて。
悪根が見てふらつくなりまするは用心をわすれ
ませ。わるうすると本心じやと思つて悪心じや
やら。我と我が手に合点がゆかず。そのくるしい
心から。おのれはくなどのうすが思ふやうにゆかぬ
ゆゑハアスウ／＼と肩で息をせねばならぬ。難儀
なものじや。せめてだまつてなとゐるならよいに
うろ何ことをくるしいせわしい腹の中の中ぐへ

ます。しかしながら算用の眼を見覚えてさへ。
事一年和高貴をして。金銀をいれありけれ
ぬく。又わしの素人分門振なりく。よしあしを
見分る手が出来ませぬくやうな御しる気で
ように碁会をなされませ。一たび本心を見覚えて
まするとき。其ときぞ十しい計の鬼畏負身
指手が出来てと出来ぬる。なぜすれば本心
のいさりのなる。手理のなら手を見えさき
ちろくぞと手理しつるは中くらけたる

-masū. Shikashi nagara, saijō no kane wo mi-oboyete mo, han-|
but best money to see-remembering even half
But even after they were well acquainted with the best money, if for

ki ichi nen hoka shōbai wo shite, kingin wo tori-atsūkawa-|nū to,
year one year other business doing gold & silver to take not to handle if
half or a whole year doing other business, they do not handle gold or silver,

mata moto no shirōto-gata dōyō ni narite, yoshi-ashi wo | mi-
again origin a non-professional in the same manner having become good bad to see
having again become like non-professionals as they originally were, it said (*i.e.*, the book)

wakuru koto ga dekimasenū to mōsaremashita.
to distinguish affair they cannot it said
that they cannot distinguish good from bad.

Kore de, | yō go gaten wo nasaremase. Hito tabi hon-
this by well comprehension one time original
By this please to understand well. When you are once

shin wo mi-oboye-|masuru to, sono ato kara, sūkoshi bakari
heart so soon as that - after - from a little only
well acquainted with the original heart, thenceforward even if only a little selfish-

no mibiiki mi-|gatte ga dekite mo, jikini shireru. Nase nareba?
selfishness being produced. even soon to be known why
ness springs up, it is soon known. Why?

Honshin | no akiraka naru muri no nai koto wo mi-oboyeta
bright to be wrong to be not
Because one has a recollection of the bright faultlessness of the original heart,

yuye, | chiyotto demo murirashii koto wa naka-naka uketsūkeru |
because . a little even fault-like thoroughly to admit of
even a little fault-resembling thing

(Notes to page 21.)

Mōsaremashita [4]. Refers apparently to the book from which the story is taken.

Mibiiki migatte [6,7] = *mi hiiki mi katte*, self-party, self-convenience. The phrase is one that frequently recurs, and simply means 'selfishness.'

Nase nareba [7] *-ba* is *wa* with the nigori, and the phrase is 'in regard to its being, Why?' or 'Why is it?' or simply 'Why?'

tada yoroshiki kane wo nichi-nichi ni mise-oki, shikato yoki kane
only good money every day to show to put fully good
displaying (before them) only good money every day, when (koro) they fully

wo | mi-oboyetaru koro, soto akugin wo misureba, tachi-machi ni |
to look to remember time stealthily if he shows sudden -ly
know good money, if one stealthily show (them) bad money, suddenly the

ashiki kane to shiru koto kagami wo terashite mono wo miru ga
bad that to know circumstance mirror causing to reflect to see
knowledge that (it is) bad money resembles the seeing an object, having caused a mirror

| gotoshi. Kore, ichi-mokŭka ni akugin to mi-kiwamuru koto wa
like unto this one glance that to see to decide
to reflect. This distinguishing at a glance that it is bad money,

saijō no | kane wo mi-oboyetaru yuye nari. Kaku no gotoku
best because to be thus like
is because they recollect the appearance of the best money. When they are taught in

oshiyuru toki wa | kono komono shōgai akugin wo mi-son-suru koto
to teach time these shop-boys life-limit to mistake
this way, these shop-boys their lives long do not mistake bad money

nashi to mō-| saretaru yoshi uketamawarimashĭta. Kono hanashi
not to be thus the saying purport have heard this story
thus I have heard. Although I know

no hongi wa | sonjimasenedomo, dōri ni oite wa naruhodo mottomo
true-false although I do not know principle really most
not whether this story is true or false, in principle this really excellent mode (kata) of

na | oshiye-kata jitsuni abunage no nai keiko de gozari-|
(naru) to teach side indeed danger not to be practice
teaching is indeed a training devoid of danger

(Notes to page 20.)

Yoroshiki [1], written form. The spoken is *yoroshiu.*
Shite, doing, is understood after *shĭkato* [1].
Yoki [1], written form. The spoken is *yoi.*
Koro [2] is for *toki*, which is the word used in the spoken language.
Akugin [2 and 4], *lit.*, bad silver, has here the sense of bad money. The French *argent* is [an exact parallel.
Ashiki [3] is again a written form.
Ashiki kane, etc. [3], *naru*, to be, understood before *to.*
Akugin [4], *naru*, to be, is understood before *to.*
Kaku and **gotoku** [5] are written forms. More *lit.*, as to the teaching-time like thus.
Kono, etc. [6], more *lit.*, these shop-boys, (their) lives long, the mistaking-circumstance of bad money is not.
To, etc. [6], more *lit.*, the saying-thus-purport, I have heard.
Ni oite [8] is simply the same as *nite*, in.
Abunage [9] *-ge* is a termination which converts an adj. into a noun. It is identical with *ki*, spirit, and thus *abunage* means the spirit of danger, *i.e.*, dangerousness.

たゞ宜しき根を築くふ入る任重。志りしられ根を
入れても手ずからるつ。ソト悪根とつくまたど忽り
ならきに根く志る事。読をくりして妙とるへるづ
ぞし。らさ一月下に悪根るん極る事へ豺上の
根をこん見てゐる中きなり。かくれぞくそしわり時へ。
この小者生涯悪根と入ん損ずるくるすなしとも
さまらるより郡くの内しき此を於しの素偽く
ぞんぜしまひのどる。五臓に於りてへ晩かど若ぶ
そくるさ。実木にづる気の芽へ松る香ぐおさう

うちに安楽をゆるしくめやまする。一度本心を御忘
く なされまするど。きのかなのものじや。ちやうどうし
この身贔屓依怙なくて直に胸へおさへまする。
あまりにはつく。なる人まくる物がらのはのぞみ。
さる商家屋の主人乃得意のなかりとて
やさしからん。商賣渡世も。金銀のよしあしを
見分るが肝要じや。そう見るけ様を小者まで
申さぬ。其家くるく遣ひまるども。この商家屋の
主人のをしへるこは始よりおしも悪銀を見せぬ

uchi, shingaku wo o süsüme-mōshimasuru. Ichido hon-shin wo
inside heart learning to persuade I say (polite) one time original heart
disease, let me persuade you to the study of morality. When once you compre-

go ye-|tokŭ nasaremasuru to, kimĭyōna mono ja. Chĭyotto shĭ-|ta
to comprehend to do when wonderful slightly done
hend the original heart, it is a wonderful thing. Even a slightly done

mibĭki migatte de mo, jĭkini mune ye kotayemasuru.
partiality selfishness even soon breast to penetrate
bias or selfishness, soon affects the breast.

Kore ni tsuite, aru hĭto mayekata mono-gatari no tsuide
this to exist man previously
Connected with this, is the thing told by a certain man in the course of old

ni | saru riyō-gaye-ya no aruji no tokui no hanashi nari tote |
certain money to change house master to be
story-telling, mentioning (tote) that it was (nari) a favourite story of the master of a cer-

mōsaretaru wa;—
the thing told
tain money-changer's shop.

Riyō-gaye tosei wa kin-gĭn no yoshi-ashi wo | mi-wakuru ga
business gold silver good bad to see to distinguish
As to the money-changing business, distinguishing the good and bad of gold and

kanyō ja. Sono mi-wake yō wo ko-mono ni oshi-|yuru ni,
essential (de aru) that to see distinguish manner shop-boy to teach
silver is essential. In teaching the shop-boys the mode of distinguishing (them),

sono iye-iye nite chigai aredomo, kono riyō-gaye-ya no | aruji
these in difference altho' there be this
altho' there be differences in various houses, as to the system of instruction of the master

no oshiye-kata wa, hajime yori sūkoshi mo akugin wo misesu |
to instruct side beginning from a little even bad silver not to show
of this money-changer's, not even in the least showing (them) bad silver from the com-
t.a. [mencement

(Notes to page 19.)

O süsüme, etc. [1], *lit.*, I say persuasion. This is the polite way of putting the first person. For the second, *nasaru* is used instead of *mōsŭ*, as may be seen in the next line. **Yetokŭ nasaremasuru** [1, 2], to do comprehension. The address is in the second person to those present, and for that reason also an honorific *go* precedes *yetokŭ*. See remarks on *surcba* p. 32. **Kimĭyōna,** etc. [2], *i.e.*, what you have attained to is a wonderful thing. **Jĭkini** etc., [3], *lit.*, soon it penetrates to, or reacts on, the breast. **Tsuite** [4], part. of *tsuku*, 'to stick.' The passage which contains this story appears to be related from a book in the written language, and many of the written forms are retained in the preacher's version. **Tsuide** [4], part. of *tsugu*, 'to join on.' **Saru** [5] *sa aru*, 'thus to be.' **Tokui no hanashi** [5]. *Tokui* is *forte*, speciality, skilfulness, and thus the phrase seems to mean that the story is one of the skilfulness of the master, one that redounded to his credit and that he was fond of telling; a story that exhibits a little boastful vanity. *Tokui no kawo*, a pleased countenance; *tokui na koto*, a thing in which one excels; *tokui no kĭyōgai*, easy circumstances; *ano hĭto wa Yokohama de hanahada tokui de gozarimasŭ*, that man is very much pleased with Yokohama. These examples show that *tokui* has many senses, and it eventually comes to mean, 'a customer,' *i.e.*, one accustomed. **Tote** [5], for *to iute*, 'thus saying.' **Mōsaretaru,** [6] written form.

gozarimasenŭ. Hitai ni suji ga tatte, ato-kara hara no tatsu no |
forehead veins having arisen afterwards belly to arise (mono)
sorrowful. It is not (that) the veins having swollen in the forehead, we (after-

de wa gozarimasenŭ. Nani-goto mo kokoro ga saki ja. Sono
what thing even front (de aru)
wards) become angry. Whatsoever it be, the heart is foremost. All

kokoro ni | omou tokoro wa mina katachi ye arawaremasuru.
to think all appearance to become manifest
the thoughts in that heart become manifest externally.

Kore wo "uchi ni makoto areba hoka ni arawaruru" to
inside truth if there be outside to become manifest
This is called (in the text) "if there be truth within, it becomes manifest without."

mōshimasŭ. Nan to, kore de mo kokoro no yugami ga |
to be distorted
What! notwithstanding this, can the deformity of the heart be a thing

kakusareru mono de gozarimashō ka.
to be hidden (future)
to be hidden?

Kuchi-gotaye mo kokoro no wadzurai, | hana-uta mo kokoro
both disease and
Both surly answers to superiors and muttering to oneself are diseases of the

no wadzurai; hayō yōjō wo itashimasenŭ | to, tachi-wadzurai wa
quickly not to do if to stand disease
heart; if you do not quickly attend to yourself, the chronic disease is

hombuku ga mutsukashii. Moshi tai-biyō ni nari-|mashite wa,
recovery difficult if great disease having become
difficult of recovery. If it becomes a grave disease,

Giba Henjaku ga haisai de mo, dō mo itashi-|kata wa gozari-
of consultation howsoever to do side is
even with a consultation of Giba and Henjaku, there is no help for it.

masenŭ. Saru ni yotte, sono tai-biyō ni naranŭ |
not that
In regard to this being so, before it becomes that grave

(Notes to page 18.)

Hara no tatsu [1]. See vocab. **Tokoro** [3], which chiefly means 'place,' sometimes, as here, signifies circumstance, and is equivalent to *koto*. *Omou tokoro*, a thinking circumstance, *i.e.*, what one thinks; *tokoro* thus supplying the place of a relative which does not exist in Japanese. (See also note p. 16.) **Kuchi-gotaye** [5], *lit.*, mouth to reply. **Hana-uta** [6], *lit.*, nose-song, trans., muttering; *tsubuyaki* seems to have a similar signification. The audience consists perhaps chiefly of women of the lower class. **Yō-jō** [6], (Chi.) fostering, the taking care of oneself generally, attention to health in diet, clothing, etc. The Japanese equivalent is *sei wo yashinau*, 'to cherish life.' The meaning is, if you do not take the disease in hand in time, it becomes chronic and then cure is difficult. There is here a transition from the heart to the body without breaking off. A common figure in Japanese. **Giba** and **Henjaku** [8]. "Famous Indian and Chinese physicians." (Mitford.) **Dō mo,** etc. [8], *lit.*, there is no how soever a doing side. **Sono,** etc. [9], *lit.*, inside the not becoming that grave disease. A common idiom.

ござりませぬ。額に字が立てゝあるはうの立の
ではござりませぬ。何ですも人がそれじやその人に
あります。皆かたちへあらはれて居る。さまを誠
於中形於外（中ニアレバ外ニアラハル）とやましますナント是でも人の心の姿が
かくされるものでござりませうか。口くらふも人の好ひ。
鼻でかぐも人の心のこのみ。茶屋で養生してありませぬ
と立ち好ひする。華嬉がありしへとし太病に茶
聞いて耆婆扁鵲が配剤でもどうかなりし
気もござりませぬ。さうまでよくある太病にありしぬ

出来ぬうちぬけて。蜘をとつておいらひこいく
とやましいざいのんが蜘蛛(くも)あつらひまいてる。飯粒(いひぶつ)へ
蜘蛛(くも)まで見てぬ。陰(うら)するより形(あと)うつてへなしじや。
こまじやによつて。人(ひと)の心(こころ)を隠(かく)されませぬ。心に
怒(いかり)があると。顔(かほ)に青(あを)すぢがたちまする。心(こころ)にかなし
いことがあると目(め)になみだがうかぶ。心にうれしいことが
あるとほうべたに笑くぼが入つて。心におかしいことがある
と。笑(わら)ひ声(こゑ)に成(なり)まする。道(こゝろ)まゐ心(こころ)よりしては数(なみ)へ
出まする。目に涙(なみだ)が出て。心がかなしうなるのぐしき

Chōkichi, nukaranū kawo de, tatami wo tataite, "Ototsui koi,
innocent fac with mats beating day before yesterday
Chokichi with an innocent face, beating the mats, said, "Come the day be-

"ototsui koi" | to mōshimashita. Nambo kumo ashirai
come said how much spider treatment
fore yesterday: come the day before yesterday." Howsoever much he may

ni shite mo, ii-dako wa | kumo ni wa miyenū.
doing soever cuttle-fish not to seem
treat them as spiders, the cuttle-fish will not look like spiders.

"Kakuretaru yori arawaruru wa nashi" ja. |
to be hidden than to be manifest not to be
It is (the saying), "Than that which is hidden that which is manifest is not (other)."

Kore ja ni yotte, hito no kokoro wa kakusaremasenū. Kokoro
man heart not to be hidden
In regard to this being so, the heart of man cannot be concealed. When

ni | ikari ga aru to, hitai ni awo-suji ga tachimasuru. Kokoro ni
anger to be when forehead blue vein to arise
there is anger in the heart, blue veins arise in the forehead. When there is

kanashi-|mi ga aru to, me ni namida ga ukaml; kokoro ni
sadness eye tear to swim
sadness in the heart, tears swim in the eyes; when there is

ureshimi ga | aru to, hōbeta ni yekubo ga iri; kokoro ni okashimi
joy cheek dimple to enter merriment
joy in the heart, dimples come in the cheeks; when there is merriment

ga aru | to, warai-gawo ni narimasuru. Kore mina kokoro yori
laughter face to become all from
in the heart, (the face) becomes a laughing face. All these being done from the

shite, kawo ye | demasuru. Me ni namida ga dete, kokoro ga
being done come out eye tear coming out
heart, come out into the face. It is not (that) tears having started in the eyes, the

kanashiu naru no de wa |
sorrowful to become (mono)
heart (afterwards) becomes

(Notes to page 17.)

Tatami [1], the rice-straw mats which are laid down in Japanese houses. **Ototsui koi** [1]. A charm used to drive away spiders. Like our children's "Rain, rain, go to Spain"; "Lady bird, lady bird, fly away home," etc. **Nambo**, etc. [2], more *lit.*, 'howsoever much doing spider-treatment, as to cuttle-fish they do not seem spiders.' Observe the force of *wa* here, contrasting the two objects, see note p. 2. **Kakuretaru** [3]. Written form of *kakureru*: the quotation is from some book. *Hoka*, 'other,' is understood before *wa*. The meaning is evident.—That which is hidden and that which is manifest are (will be) the same. Nothing remains concealed. Murder will out. *Tout se sait.* **Kakusaremasenū** [4], neg. pass. of *kakusareru* 'to be hidden (by some one)', used as a potential. *Kakureru*, 'to be,' or 'remain, hidden'; *kakusu* 'to hide (anything).' **Kokoro ni.........narimasuru** [5 to 8] This is an excellent example of the rule in Japanese syntax,—"When two or more verbs are co-ordinated in the same sentence, the last only receives the inflection which properly belongs to all, those which precede "being placed in the root form" (Aston's *Written Grammar*, p. 31). Here *ukanni* and *iri* are roots, while *narimasuru* is the present tense. **Kanashi-mi** [5], **ureshi-mi** [6], **okashi-mi** [7]. These are all adjectival roots with the termination *-mi* which forms the derived noun. **No** [9] need not be translated. More *lit.*, *kanashiu naru no* is 'a sorrowful-become thing.' The idiom is one of the commonest in Japanese.

"koitsŭ wa uma-sōna mono ga tanto aru; suzuri-buta wa tama-|go
dainty like plenty to be lacquer tray egg
"As to these here, there are plenty of dainties; the lacquer-tray, (was) an

"no maki-yaki, tatta hĭto-kire haka nokotte nai. Yō kū | kiyaku
roll roast merely one slice left not to be well to eat guest
"omeletto, there is not left other than one slice merely. Well-eating guests

"ja. Koitsŭ wa nan ja? Ha, ha-a! kama-boko ja sō-|na" to,
(de aru) (de aru) (de aru) like
"they are! As to this here, what is it? Ha! it is like a baked mince of fish," thus (think-

hĭto-kire tsumande kuchi ye hōbari, katawara wo mireba |
mouth side when he saw
ing), taking up a slice (and) stuffing it into his mouth, when he looked aside there are

ii-dako ga nanatsŭ yatsŭ Nankin no domburi no naka ni kuruma-
seven eight bowl middle wheel
seven or eight cuttle-fish seated in a circle in a Nankin bowl,

za ni | zasen shĭte iru. "Koitsŭ wa yerai" to, tsumamu
seat doing to remain choice
lost in meditation. "This here is choice!" thus (thinking), just as he was

tokoro ye | danna no ashi-oto,—— "Kore de wa naranŭ" to,
master foot sound this
picking it up, the footsteps of (his) master!—— "This will never do!" thus (thinking),

tamoto ye oshi-komi, | chōshi saka-dzuki wo utsubuite toru, hiyōshi
sleeve to thrust to put in stooping to take
thrusting (it) into (his) sleeve, stooping he takes the sake bottle and cups, just as

ni ii-dako ga tamoto | kara koro-goro to,—— danna me-bayaku,
from roll roll eye-swiftly
(he) does so, the cuttle-fish rolling from (his) sleeve,—— the master quick-eye'd-ly (says)

"Sore wa nan ja?" |
"What is that?"

(Notes to page 16.)

Koitsŭ [1, 3, 6], vulg. for *kore*, 'these,' trans. 'these here.' **Haka** [2], vulgar pronunciation of *hoka*, 'other.' **Yō**, etc. [2, 3]. The absence of honorifics shows that Chōkichi was in no pleased mood with his master's guests. **Sōna to** [3, 4]. *Omōte*, 'thinking,' is understood. **Tsumande** [4] for *tsumamite*, part. of *tsumamu* (line 6), 'to pinch, to take up with the finger and thumb.' **Hōbari** [4], *hō hari; lit.*, cheek-to-stretch. **Ii-dako** [5]. *Ii*, 'boiled rice,' *tako*, 'cuttle-fish.' A dish of the two combined. **Zazen** [6], 'meditation.' A term used by the Zenshū sect of Buddhists. The preacher indulges in a little jocular profanity. **Kuruma-za**, etc. [5, 6], *lit.*, remain doing *zazen* in a wheel-seat. **Yerai** [6], used here in the way in which we say "This is jolly." **To** [6]. *Omōte*, 'thinking,' understood. **Tokoro** [6] here used for 'occasion.' It more generally means 'spot' or 'place'; *tsumamu tokoro ye*, 'at the picking up occasion, *i.e.*, just as he was picking it up. See also note p. 18. **Danna no ashi-oto** [7]. The sentence breaks off abruptly, leaving the impression of surprise, as we might say, When, lo! the master's footsteps. **Naranŭ** [7], *lit.*, does not become; the idiom. form for, 'must not be,' 'will not do,' etc. **Chōshi** [8], a porcelain *sake* bottle. **Sakadzuki** [8], shallow cups from which *sake* (which becomes *saka* in compos.) is drunk. **Hiyōshi** [8], beating time to music. As it were, in unison with his stooping to take the sake-bottle. Trans. 'just as he does.' **Koro-goro** [9], an adverb; *koro* repeated with the nigori. Another instance of a figurative breaking off in the middle of the sentence, which perhaps might be completed thus, *koro-goro to shĭte korobu*, *i.e.*, rollingly (to coin a word) doing it rolls down.

あらつハ味(うま)さうなるものがたんとある。硯(すゞり)ぶたハ鶉
卵(ご)の巻焼(まきやき)。タッタ一ト切(ひときれ)なりともくなへ。よく喰
客(きやく)じや。あらつを何(なん)じや。ハア蒲(かま)ぼこじややさう
なく。ひと切(きれ)をまんぐ口(くち)へほうばり。側(うつろ)をうれしが。
飯蛸(いひだこ)が七ツ八ツ。南京(なんきん)のどんぶりの中に車蝦(くるまえび)が、
座禅(ざぜん)してゐる。あらつをみれバはまぐりさゞへ。
只椀(ずんな)のおし音(おと)。あまでなしがく頬へおかしさ。
銚子(てうし)盃(さかづき)を腕(うで)ぐらくとる拍子(ひやうし)に飯蛸(いひだこ)のちれたれて
ゝ。あらくを只椀(ずんな)用(や)でやくざつまハ何(なん)じや

くるしうござんや。此無縁別かうおあるうすじや。是
じやからよつく此しも沖のハかりませぬ。なるほどの
尽未どのが。碁所に居眠してゐる長吉をよび起
し〳〵。コレ長吉。御客さまがあつて御奥へ呼なされるぞ。
奥にある酒やさかなを。碁所へはこんだがよい。長
吉。目をこすりながら。ふせうぶしやうに返事しながら。
奥へ往て。そろ〳〵とつまみぐひ。硯蓋の中から小鉢の中。
うまいものゝ勢ぞろへ。こゝらへものじや。権が旨
菊もせぬに。目の玉がくる〳〵と淡き出しますんじや

kurushiu nai to, kono mufumbetsu kara okoru koto ja. Kore |
painful not to be this non-discrimination from to arise affair (de aru)
bent, even being twisted; it arises from this want of discrimination. Because

ja ni yotte, sūkoshi mo yudan wa narimasenū.
(de aru) a little even negligence " does not become
this is the case, there ought not to be even a particle of negligence.

Aru tokoro no | danna dono ga dai-dokoro ni i-nebutte iru
to exist place master Mr. kitchen dozing to be
The master of a certain place calling up Chōkichi (who was) dozing in the kitchen

Chōkichi wo yobi-oko-|shite, "Kore! Chōkichi; o kyakū sama ga
calling up guest gentleman
(says), "Here! Chōkichi; the guests have already

mō o kayeri nasareta: | oku ni aru sake ya sakana wo dai-kokoro
already to return have pleased to do back to be wine or fish kitchen
departed: the having carried the wine or fish (that) are in the back

ye hakonda ga yoi." Chō-|kichi, me wo kosuri-gosuri,
into having carried good eye to rub
(part of the house) into the kitchen, is good." Chōkichi rubbing his eyes,

fusho-busho ni henji shi nagara, | oku ye itte, sokora wo
unwilling -ly answer to make whilst having gone thereabouts
having gone to the back (of the house) whilst unwillingly answering, when he looked

mireba susuri-buta yara kobachi yara, | umai mono no sei-zoroye
when he saw a lacquer tray or little bowl sweet the display
round, what with lacquer trays, what with little bowls, the display of dainties—

—(kowai mono ja!)—Tare ga sai-|soku mo senū ni, me no tama
terrible (de aru) anyone instigation not to do ball
(what a terrible thing it is!)—Without anyone's instigation, rolling about

ga kiyoro-tsuki-dashi, "Nan ja? |
rolling about
(his) eyeballs, "What is this?

(Notes to page 15.)

To (*omōte*, thinking, understood) translated last page by, 'thinking that.'
Okoru koto ja [1], *lit.*, it is an arising affair, *i.e.*, the mistake of attending to the body and not to the heart.
Oku, etc. [5], *i.e.*, you had better take the wine, etc.
Kosuri-gosuri [6]; *shite*, doing, is understood.
When **nagara** [6] is employed with a verb, it is always attached to the root form.
Susuri-buta [7]. The nigori here is a vulgarity. It should be *susuri-futa*.
Tare ga [8], more *lit.*, as to (the) anyone's not doing even instigation.
Kiyoro-tsuki-dashi [9], see note p. 8.
Nan ja [9] (for *nani de aru*), what is it?

sewa shĭte yaru to, metta ni ureshigatte naosŭ: kokoro no |
trouble doing to give if extremely joyful-feeling to mend heart
for his body, feeling much pleased he amends (it): if there is a

sewa wo suru hĭto ga aru to, makkuro ni natte, hara wo
to do man to be if very black having become belly
man to take trouble for (his) heart, having become very black, getting into a

tate, | sono kokoro wo naosō to senŭ wa, dō iu hiyōshi no
setting up that will mend not to do how to call harmony
passion, (his) not amending (his) heart, from a how-called mistake

machi-|gai de, kore hodo made mayōta mono de gozarimashō
mistake from this quantity as far as gone astray thing can it be
in harmony, can so great an error arise?

zo? | Kore wa yoso no koto de wa nai. O tagai ni, tai
this elsewhere affair not to be you & I to more
This is not the affair of others. To all of us, more

ka shō ka, | iro kaye shina kaye, konna machigai wa yete
or less this sort error getting (at)
or less, in all ways, this sort of error is apt to occur.

aritagaru | mono de gozarimasŭ. Yō go gimmi wo nasarimase.|
well examination please to do
Examine well (into this).

Kore ga kore, katachi wa hĭto no me ni kakaredomo,
this appearance men eyes altho' it affects
It is this, because although outward appearance strikes,

kokoro wa hĭto no | me ni kakaranŭ yuye, yugande atte mo,
not to affect because bent being even
the heart does not strike men's eyes, thinking that it is not

magatte atte mo, |
twisted
distressing even being

(Notes to page 14.)

Koto sewa shĭte [1], more *lit.*, affair-trouble doing.
To [1]; *sureba*, if one does, is understood.
Kokoro etc. [1 etc.] More intelligibly, What can we call the discordant condition of mind which gives rise to such an error as not alone not amending one's faults when they are pointed out, but also working oneself into a passion at the very suggestion.
Hara wo tate [2], see vocab.
Kore hodo made [4], translate, 'so great,' 'so much'
Mayōta mono [4], a going astray, an error.
De gozarimashō [4]. The future often has a potential meaning. *De* marks the predicate.
Zo [4], an emphatic particle.
O tagai ni etc. [5] The sentence is somewhat of a *crux*, but the interlinear translation is offered. *Aritagaru* seems to be for *aritaki aru*, to be desirous, to be apt to.
Kore wa etc. [5] that is to say, it concerns ourselves closely.
Iro kaye shina kaye [5], *lit.*, colour change, article change, an idiomatic expression meaning, 'in all ways.'
Yō go etc. [7, etc.] more freely, Examine well into the cause of this mistake. It is the following: outward appearances strike our eyes, but the heart does not, and therefore we do not consider the deformity of the heart to be distressing. It is from this want of discrimination that the mistake arises.

世話(せわ)して貰ふと滅多(めつた)にうましがつくものです。心(こころ)の
せまいことをする人があると窮屈(きうくつ)なりて損(そん)をとる。
その人を中(なか)さうとせねばならぬ拍子(ひやうし)の間(ま)ち
がひで。手(て)ほどまで迷(まよ)つてしまうのでございますぞ。
ひろくよその事(こと)ぢやないなんど。お互(たが)ひに大損(ぞんらう)小損(しやうそん)。
いろいろしまじまあんまりさちがひは得(え)くあるさうな
ものでございます。ようは吟味(ごぎんみ)をなさりませ。
気(け)がつきぬ素人(すまひ)は人(ひと)の目(め)にかゝりまども。ところ人の
目(め)につくらぬ見え。ゆがんで有(あ)つても使(つか)つて有ても

申する。軍兵まで兵隊まで勇ましう覚悟を正して。
コレハく御気を惜しき千万動ぜんずる。彼れ
まも相応の御用もござりますべからずでござらうや
嬉しきうる新しく挨拶せられまして。きみらが待ち
かく。時に軍を兵隊どの。足下の御心御座りまして
その上にますまいぬ。チトらを正当に御持かきまし。心の
ゆだんだうしてあまりあんぐらしうあぐらとゆふさう。
ごうまゐりてうしろぞ。刀にその身に従ひしく。
忽ち刃傷にあうてこうけるナント人をかつぐのを

"masuru." **Gunda-Bei shikatsūberashu kata-ginu wo tadashite |**
-pear precisely shoulder silk having adjusted
Gunda-Bei having adjusted his coat with great nicety

"Kore wa, kore wa, o ki wo tsukerare, sen-ban katajikenō
this this mind 1,000 10,000 grateful
"Ah, I see, I feel infinitely obliged (to you) for noticing it.

"sonsuru. Nani nari | to mo, sō-ō no go yō mo gozaraba,
to think what to be even suitable service even if there should be
"If there should be any, be it what it may, suitable service (for you) I

"uketamawaru de gozarō" to, | ureshi-sōna kawo shite aisatsu seraruru.
to listen will be joyful like face making reply to make
"will attend to it," thus (saying) forming a pleased countenance, he makes reply.

Koitsū ga machiga-|ute;— "Toki ni, Gunda-Bei dono, sokka
This fellow time in you
If this fellow differing: "By the bye Mr. Gunda-Bei, I cannot

"no go shinjutsu hanahada motte | sono i yemasenū; chito kokoro
heart that meaning not to get a very little
"make out the meaning of your heart at all; be so good as to

"wo shōjiki ni o mochi nasare; kokoro no | yugami ga miyete
upright -ly to hold distortion being visible
"keep it a little honest; the depravity of the heart being visible is

"hanahada migurushu gozaru" to iutara, | dō suru de arō so?
very painful to see is if he said how to do will be
"very painful to see," thus had said, what would he do?

Katana ni sori-utte, tsuba uchi-narashi, | tachimachi ninjō ni oyobu
sword (vocab.) guard (vocab.) immediately sword-edge to come to
Turning up the back of his sword, noisily slamming the guard, immediately it will come to a

de arō.
will be
sword fight.

Nanto, hito wa, karada no koto |
mankind body affair
Well! well! as to man, if one takes trouble

(Notes to page 13.)

Ki wo tsukerare [1], *lit.*, to apply the mind. Pass. voice used as an honorif.
Sen-ban, etc. [2], *lit.*, ten million grateful I think.
Nani nari to, etc. [2]. *Shite*, doing, is understood after *to*.
Uketamawaru de gozarō [3], *lit.*, to listen (the listening) will be. The honorifics *go*, *gozaraba*, *gozarō*, are sufficient without employing a pronoun of the first or second persons.
Second **To** [3]. *Iute*, saying, is understood.
Seraruru [4], honorific form for *suru*.
Koitsu [4], nom. to *iutara* [7]. "If this fellow differing.........thus had said."
Machiga-|ute [4, 5], *machigōte* necessarily written thus to show the division of the lines; *au* = *ō*, see General Notes.
Hanahada motte [5], an adverbial phrase, *lit.*, very much taking. The sense is more *lit.*, your heart, very much I do not get its meaning.
Hito wa [9], the force of *wa* is well exemplified here. See note, p. 2.

"konjō wa shibutoi konjō ja; chitto fukure-dzura yame | nasare"
disposition sullen (de aru) a little to puff out cease
"disposition is a sullen disposition; be good enough to give over pouting a little,"

to iutara, o San don ga nan to iu de arō zo? | Chito
had said Miss to say will be a little
thus if he had said, what *would* Miss San say? Reflect-

kangayete, gorōjimase. "Ata! name-kūsatta kodettchi (detsu-|chi)-
reflecting look (interjection) (see vocab.) little apprentice
ing a little, be so good as to look. "What! (you) conceited little apprentice face!

"dzura! Washi ga kokoro ga yugande arō ga, san kaku ni
I of heart distorted 3 corner
My heart may be depraved, it may have be-

"natte | arō ga, onore ga sewa ni naru mono ka? Onore
having become you of trouble to become thing ? yourself
come three-cornered, but has it anything to do with you? Mind

"oboye-|te ketsukare! Shō-ben tarete mo futon no sen-daku wa
remembering (see vocab.) even mattress the washing
"your own business! Even when you make your water, I wo'n't wash (your)

"shite | yari wa senū" to, tsuno no hayenū oni no yōni nari-
doing to give not to do horn not to grow devil like to
"mattress for you," thus (saying) she becomes a devil without the horns.

masuru. | Kore wa o San don no koto bakari ja nai.
become this affair only (de wa) not to be
This is not Miss San's affair only.

"Iya! nani! Gunda | Bei dono o kami-shimo no go mon
ah! why! Mr. (see vocab.) cognisance
"Hola! Mr. Gunda-Bei, the cognisance on your costume appears a little o' one

"ga sūkoshi kata-yotte miye-|
a little side approaching to ap-
"side."

(Notes to page 12.)

Dzura [1, 4] is *tsura* with the nigori. The word is never used but in a bad sense, as 'phiz;' *kawo* is correct. **Iutara** [2] for *iutareba*. **Nan to,** etc. [2] *lit.*, 'to say that what, will she be?' *Nan* for *nani*. *De* marks the predicate. *Arō*. The future very frequently has a potential signification. See also lines 4 & 5. *Zo*, an emphatic particle translated by putting "*would*" in italics. **San** [2]. The Chinese character for San here shows that, like many Japanese names, it is translateable. It is simply, Three. **Chito** [3] same as *Chitto* [1]. **Gorōjimase** [3]. See vocabulary. Look, that is, see and think what she would be likely to say. **Name-kūsatta** [3], *lit.* raw-rotten. Rotten before he's ripe. Reminds one of *petit crevé*. **Ko-dettchi-dzura** [3,4]. As Charlotte might call Oliver Twist "Workus." **Washi** [4] vulgarly for *Watakūshi*. **Ga** [4,5]. The first *ga* in this sentence is the sign of the genitive case, so is the fifth; the second denotes that *kokoro* is the nominative to *arō*; in the third and fourth instances *ga* has the force of, although it is not quite equal to 'but.' **Onore ga sewa,** etc. [5], more *lit.*, Is it a thing that becomes your trouble? Is it to be a trouble to you? I wo'n't trouble you to mend it! **Ketsukare** [6] is an insulting auxiliary used in the same way as the polite auxiliaries *nasare* and *kudasare*. **Sen-daku,** etc. [6, 7]. *Sen*, to wash, is Chinese; *arau* is the Japanese verb. *Daku* is *taku* with the nigori. There is an idiomatic piling up of verbs here; more *lit.*, The washing of the mattress doing, I will not do the bestowal. *Yari wa senū* is a strong negative for *yaranū*. **To** [7], *Iute*, saying, is understood. **Tsuno,** etc. [7], *lit.*, She becomes in the manner *(yō)* of a not-growing-of-horns devil. The Japanese devil, like our own, is represented with horns. **O and go** [9], Honorifics.

猿猴(えんこう)はまづこへ猿猴(えんこう)じや。チツトふくまばかりやめ
なされしといふてか。三どんが何(なん)とつゞであらうぞ。
チト考(かんが)へて御(ご)らうじ御(ご)せ。あさなあさな小(こ)丁
稚(ち)づら。まゝしが心(こゝろ)が白げんでいふが。三角(さんかく)に成(なつ)て
いろいろが。お乃ゝが世話(せわ)になるその訳。私(わたし)のまゝ覚(おぼえ)
てからまで。小便(しようべん)までをさも。ふとんの洗濯(せんだく)へして
やりはせぬと。角(つの)のはえぬ鬼(おに)の猿(まう)にぬまされ。
らまはおさんどんのするだらうじやあるまへ。イヤ左軍(えんさ)を
多衛(ごん)どの。御上下(おかみしも)の御役(ごりれ)が。すましてゐるくまつて人く

たると。指のさきに手拭をまいて顔じゆうをのま
が鼻の先をなでる後藤が目貫をみがくやうに。
そこら中拭ぐりまはして。長吉どん。モウよさ
さく。イヤ〳〵ほんぐさの如く鎖斗になつた。ドレ〳〵
水でもこ小袖ふ裾をうつし〳〵掃除してお
ぶろ。おさんどんの申すに。アノ長吉どんは了和らく
いふども気じや。晩乃お茶を柄子。ゆうがくお礼
やさしやなさまへと。銭多ふうまつしつく。礼と
いふ。そく此長吉どのが。コレ〳〵おさんどんお主への

"aru?" to, yubi no saki ni tenugui wo maite, hĭtai-guchi de
finger tip towel having rolled
"sticking?" thus (saying) rolling a towel round the end of her finger, looking steadily

onore | ga hana no saki wo nagame, Gotō ga menuki wo horu yō
oneself of nose to look steadily to carve manner
with the front of the forehead at the tip of her nose, twisting round (the towel) thereabouts

ni | sokora-ju hine-kuri-mawashite: "Chōkichi don, mō tore-|ta
in twisting round Mr. already
like Gotō carving the ornament of a sword-handle (she says) "Chōkichi, has it by this time been

ka ye?" "Iya, iya, hōbeta no kata ye yokei ni natta." "Dore,
? cheek quarter towards more than ever has become
removed?" "Ah! ah! it has gone more than ever towards the cheek." "Which!

dore, | dokoni?" to, midsu-kagami ni kawo wo utsushite sōji shĭte
water mirror face having reflected cleansing making
which! where?" thus (saying), having reflected her face in the surface of (some) water,

go-|zaru. O San don no kokoro ni wa: "Ano Chōkichi don
is Miss heart that Mr.
she cleanses (it). As to what is in Miss San's heart:— "That Mr. Chōkichi is a

"wa kawairashi-|i kodomo shu ja. Ban no o kasu wo
loveable boy person (de aru) evening
loveable boy. I must thank him when I

"shakŭshi-atari de o rei | mōsaniya narumai" to, metta ni
wooden ladle thanks
serve the evening meal," thus (thinking), feel-

ureshigatte, rei wo | iu. Moshi kono Chōkichi dono ga:
joyful feeling thanks to say Mr.
ing exceedingly joyful, she speaks (her) thanks. If this Mr. Chōkichi had said:

"Kore, kore, o San don, omaye no |
this this
"Look here, Miss San, your

(Notes to page 11.)

To [1] *Iute*, saying, understood. **Hĭtai-guchi** [1]. The expresion is humorous and vulgar. *Hĭtai* is forehead, and the compound means, front of the forehead. She leans forward to get a better sight of her nose. First **ga** [2] has the same signification as *no*. The second has the ordinary office of denoting the nominative. **Gotō** [2]. "A famous gold and silver smith of the olden time. A Benvenuto Cellini among the Japanese. His mark on a piece of metal-work enhances its value ten-fold." (Mitford.) **Menuki** [2]. Ornaments of the sword handle. They are often of minute and beautiful workmanship. Hence Miss San is said to rub her nose as carefully as Gotō, a celebrated workman, would carve one of these *menuki*. **Sokora-ju** [3]. *Sokora*, 'there'; *ju*, 'within,' is often, like *ra*, used loosely as a plural; it also gives to an adverb a more general meaning; trans., thereabouts. **Ye** [4], a particle often found after interrogatives. Resembles the English, 'Eh!' It must not be confounded with the prep. *ye*, 'towards.' **Hōbeta** [4] is vulgar; *hō* is more correct. **To** [5] *Iute*, saying, understood. *To* may in such a case be rendered by, thus. **Wa** [6]. Observe the force of the particle, which is much more strongly marked in the first than in the second instance in this line. **O kasu** [7]. Vegetables or anything else eaten with rice; *Sai* is another term. Miss San is so pleased with Chōkichi that she, even in her thoughts of him, twice uses the honorific *O* in this sentence. **Shakŭshi-atari de** [7]. *Ataru* is to hit the target; *atari* thus comes to mean vicinity in place or time, as *ju go nichĭ atari*, 'about the 15th.' The phrase under note thus is literally, 'at the wooden-ladle time.' She will then thank Chōkichi by serving him well. **To** [8] is followed by *omōte*, thinking, understood. **Metta ni** [8] is an intensitive adverb, with a variety of significations. Here trans., exceedingly.

Kokoro ga magatte atte wa, iro wa shirok'arō ga, hana-suji wa |
heart bent being complexion white may be nose line
In case of the heart's being depraved, the complexion may be white, the profile of the

tōtte arō ga, hayegiwa ga utsŭkushĭk'arō ga, sore wa | mise-
the hair line beautiful that appear-
nose may be well drawn, the boundary line of the hair may be elegant, but these being only

kake bakari de, nani no yaku ni tatanŭ koto; makiye no |
ance only what gold lacquer
external, are circumstances of no value; it is as if horse-

ju-bako ni ŭma no kŭso itta yōna mono ja. Kore wo | "hon
nest of boxes horse dung entered sort (de aru) this real
dung was in a nest of gold lacquer boxes. This is what we call

"no mi-kake-dōshi" to mōshimasŭ.
to call
"an unmistakeable deception."

Meshitaki no o San dono ga | nagashi-moto de nabe no
cook sink place (nite) pot
Miss San the cook is washing the bottoms of her pots at

shiri wo arōte iru. Dettchi no Chō-|kichi ga soba ye kite:
bottom washing to remain apprentice beside towards coming
the sink. Chōkichi the apprentice coming beside (her):

"O San don, omaye no hana no saki ni | sŭmi ga tsuite aru;
you nose end ink sticking to be
"Miss San there's ink sticking to the end of your nose;

"mitomunai" to oshiyete kureru. | O San don wa ureshigatte:
ugly warning to be pleased to do joyful-feeling
it is ugly," thus he informs (her). Miss San, feeling pleased:

"Sōka ye, doko ni tsuite |
where
"Is it so? where is it

(Notes to page 10.)

Shirok'arō ga [1]. The *u* of *shirokŭ* lost before another vowel. *Ga* has not its most ordinary signification. Here it resembles, but has not quite the force of, 'but.'

Tōtte [2] for *torite*, part. of *tōru*, to pass through from one place to another.

Bakari de [3], *atte*, being, understood.

Yakŭ ni tatanŭ [3], more lit., not to stand to use, an idiom, phrase meaning, 'useless.' *Yō (or yaku) ni tatsŭ* is the opposite, 'useful.' *De aru* is understood at the end of this clause.

Itta [4] for *irita*. *Iri* is represented by a Chinese character in the text, and the hiragana *-ta* added.

Hon no [5] an adj. qualifying *mi-kake-dōshi*.

人がまゞつて有てさ。色の白かつたが。鼻すぢへ
母つくあまりがたえ際からひかりかゝりが丈へ
ことせられたりしく。竹乃やうなものね半。前様の
こまんね小馬乃糞へさゆうなことのじや。あとを
ちんのことうけ例しとやますす飯さきのおさんどのが。
なかしりもで鶏の尻とおしつてある。丁稚の長
吉が袖へ来て。おさんどん此方人の鼻乃さき小
異がはなくある。ことしもあつておろくろくる。
おさんどんへ嫉しがつて。そうへどちよ 舟て

ませ。焼（やき）そのに何（なん）乃生根（おこん）があつたもの。是ばかりの僅（わづか）
な手（て）でも。ちよときずひとつとても。丈夫に何ぞや指（ゆび）
の歪（ゆが）みたのを恥（はづ）かしう思（おもは）く。心（こころ）のまがりは苦（く）にせ
ぬ。ぬすむかと。人をすてゝもとるとやらのじや。
さるによつて孟子（まうし）も此之謂（コレヲイフ）不知類（ルイヲシラズト）と仰せられ
なされた。ナント人は能（よ）くもてるものじやござ
りませぬか。古歌（こうか）に「かくれても深山（みやま）がくれの朽（くち）
木（き）なれば心（こころ）は花（はな）になさばなりなん」指（ゆび）や足（あし）がかく
あるも手（て）じやござりませぬ。皆心（こころ）乃ありよぢや。

-mase. Yaki-mono ni nan no ikon ga aru mono? Kore hodo
roasts what of ill-will to be thing this size
What ill-will is there in roasts? Even in the case

no wadsuka | na koto demo, shō wo kirai dai wo toru. Sore
trifling (naru) thing even small to hate great to select that
of a this-size trifling thing, one hates the small and chooses the great. That

ni, nanzoya yubi | no magatta no wo hadzukashu oboyete,
in something or other finger being bent (mono) ashamed feeling
being so, feeling ashamed at your finger having become somewhat or other bent,

kokoro no magari wa ku ni | naranū to iu wa, dai wo
heart distortion as to anxiety not to become to say
(but) as to the distortion of the heart, the fact that it turns not to anxiety, is called

sutete shō wo toru to mōsu mono ja. | Saru ni yotte, Mōshi
throwing away to call thing (de aru.)
throwing away the great and choosing the small. In reference to this being so, Mencius

mo "Kore wo tagui wo shirazu to iu" to o shikari | nasareta.
too class not to know to reprove has been pleased
too has uttered this reproof, "This is what is called being ignorant of classes."

Nanto hito wa yō urotayeta mono ja goza-|rimasenūka? Ko-ka
mankind well been bewildered (de wa) is not old poetry
What (think you)? Is not man a thing that has been quite bewildered? In the

ni "Katachi koso mi-yama-gakure no kuchi-|ki nare,
outward appearance deep mountain to be hidden a decayed tree to be
old poetry, "The exterior and that alone is a decayed tree in a deep mountain-recess,

"kokoro wa, hana ni nasaba, nari nan." Yubi ya ashi ni
heart flower if caused to be to become leg
as to the heart, if caused to flower, it blossoms perfectly." This is not a matter

kaka-|watta koto ja gozarimasenū. Mina kokoro no koto ja. |
related to all
concerning the finger or the leg. It is all the affair of the heart.

(Notes to page 9.)

Nanzoya [2], qualifies *magatta*. **Tagui wo shirazu** [5]. See the notes to page 1. **Nan to** [6]. *Omou ka* is understood. **Gozarimasenūka** [6, 7]. The *ka* is not *kana* but a Chinese character.

The sonnet quoted [7, 8] is in the written language, and the forms and grammar thus differ from the spoken language of the sermon itself. It may best be written down as follows in English letters:—

Katachi koso (5)
Mi-yama-gakure no (7)
Kuchiki nare; (5)
Kokoro wa, hana ni (7)
Nasaba, nari nan. (7)

The number of syllables is marked at the end of each line; in the last the final *n* counts as a syllable. For some excellent observations on Japanese poetry the student is referred to the Introduction to Léon de Rosny's *Anthologie Japonaise*. **Katachi,** etc. [7]. Here, as is essential to the excellence of a Japanese sonnet, there is a double signification throughout, *katachi* being both the body of man and the exterior of the tree, while *kokoro* stands for the heart of both. After **koso** [7], a selective particle of strong emphasis, *nare*, the written perfect form, is used instead of *naru*. (Aston's *Written Grammar*, p. 36.) **Nan** [8] after the root of a verb is the future of *nuru*, *inuru* (Aston's *Written Grammar*, p. 65, etc). It implies thoroughness in the action denoted by the verb; *yuku*, 'to go'; *yuki nan*, 'to go away'; *naru*, 'to become'; *nari nan*, 'to become quite.' Here *hana ni nari nan* means 'blossoms perfectly.' *Nan* is commonest in poetry.

adzukaru toki, honzen ga deru ato kara, yaki-mono wo hiite |
to receive time to come out after , from to roast thing
of receiving a feast, from after the appearance of the chief dish, as soon as they pass round

mawaru to haya, me no tama ga kiyoro-tsŭki-dashi, mukō | sangen
to go round when soon eye ball
the roasts, rolling out the eye-balls, glaring round at the

riyō donari wo nirami-mawashi, waga yaki-mono to | mi-kurabete,
both neighbour to glare at. caus. of mawaru one's own to see comparing
three opposite and the right and left neighbours, comparing (theirs) with one's own (piece

tonari no yakimono ga go roku bu hodo okii to, |
5 6 tenth quantity large if
of the) roast, if a neighbour's piece of roast (be) 5 or 6 tenths larger,

kanshakŭ ga mune ni tsuppari, "Kore no teishu wa nanto
rage breast to swell out here master what
rage swelling out in the breast, "What can the master of this house be

kokoro-|yete iru zo? Taro-Bei mo o kiyakŭ, ore mo o kiyakŭ
thinking of to be guest I also
thinking of? Taro-Bei is a guest, I also am a guest.

ja. | Nande ore ni wa chiisai yaki-mono wo tsŭketa no ja?|
(de aru) why I to small given (mono) (de aru)
Why is a small piece of roast given to me?

"Nanzo kore ni wa ishu ikon demo aru koto ka?" to, | hara no
something this in object ill-will even to be ? belly
"Is there not some object or ill-will in this? thus (saying) the

uchi ga nejire-dasŭ. Yō omōte go-rōji- |
inside to wriggle well considering look
inside of his belly begins to wriggle. Be so good as to reflect.

(Notes to page 8.)

Honzen [1], the chief table at an entertainment, trans., chief dish or *pièce de resistance*. **Hiite** [1] for *hikite*, part. of *hiku*, lit. 'to draw': extends its meaning when used in this way. *Kuwashi wo hiku*, to pass round the dessert. *Hiite mawaru* may be translated here 'pass round.' **Kiyoro-tsuki-dashi** [2], one of the long compound verbs common in Japanese. *Tsŭki* is 'to apply' (root); *kiyoro-tsŭki*, 'to stare about.' *Dashi* is the root of *dasu*, caus. of *deru*, 'to come out,' which is often added in compound verbs, as *ji wo mi-dashita*, 'I have found the character;' *medzŭrashi koto kiki-dashita*, 'I have heard (found out by hearing) a strange thing.' Here the long verb is an intensitive for 'to roll the eyes.' **Mukō** [2], to be opposite to. **Sangen** [3], lit. three houses; the phrase is borrowed from town life; *riyō tonari* being 'your neighbours' right and left,' and *mukō sangen* 'the three opposite houses.' **Donari** [3] *d* = *t* with the nigori for euphony. **Bu** [4] tenths, also means 'part.' It is used to express the denominator in fractions, as, 'one-third,' *sam bun no ichi* or *sam bu ichi*, 'of three parts, one.' **Okii** [4]. The Japanese adj. has no degrees of comparison. *Go roku*, etc., lit. is 'five (or) six tenths quantity large,' but the meaning is obvious. **Zo** [6], a particle of emphasis. **Taro Bei** [6]. So pronounced. At full length, Taro-Biyoye. Taro is a very common family name, and Biyoye, which here takes the nigori for euphony, is equally common as a pre- (or rather post-) name. John Smith is the English equivalent. **To** [8] *Iute*, saying, is understood. **Nejire-dasŭ** [9]. The *dasŭ* here in compos. conveys the idea of commencement. It has not always this force, see note supra. **Hara no,** etc. [9], *i.e.* he begins to be disturbed in himself. It must be remembered that the Japanese use 'heart' and 'belly,' etc., where we would say 'mind' and 'head,' etc., believing the seat of intelligence to be in the abdomen. **Yō,** etc. [9], more lit. well considering, be so good as to look. See vocab.

ちゞるとき。御膳が出るとちやつと焼物を引く
まはるやつらや目の玉がまはつてはき出し向
三献あとなりをみとゞけ済し。早く焼ものと
いふてくれべい。僧のやき物が又余所より大きいと。
行脚が云はしつたり。寺の亭主の何くん
なくいはるぞ。寺の主僧も和尚さまもおなじや。
なんでおまへんちつさい焼ものをはけくのぶや。
何ぞおまへん。色紙半銭でも一の年程と。
寺乃中が俗じまし出す。能うおのゝく恐らうし

魚のやうなんと持く。恥かしい事を思はず。からだから吟味して。あざるべきは所から間違ふてくるものやら。此間違ひをいふてござりますとつんとして。指不若人則知悪之。心不若人則不知悪。此之謂不知類と孟子も仰せらるゝ。是を思ふて、つるんとあらぬのじや。大を捨て小をとるやうなものでござります。人情は一般。小はきらひ。大はすき。好ひはきらひ。手ひはすきじや。ソコデ親類縁者へまでうたて。御無沙汰に

karasu no yōna kokoro wo motte, hadzukashii to mo omowasu,
crow sort heart having shameful even not to think
having a crow's sort of heart, not feeling shame,

ka-|rada bakari gimmi shite gozaru wa dō iu tokoro kara | ma-
body only examination making the being how to call place from hav-
as to the examining the body alone from a how-called-place, having

chigōte kita yara?
ing mistaken it is come
mistaken, has it come?

Kono machigai wa furū aru koto | to miyete, "Yubi hito ni
This mistake anciently to exist matter seeming
This mistake seeming to have existed of old time,

"**shikazaru toki wa, kore wo nikumu koto wo shiru. Kokoro**
"**hito ni shikazaru toki wa, sunawachi nikumu koto wo shirazu.**
"**Kore wo tagui wo shirazu to iu," to Mōshi mo ōserare-|ta.**
thus too
Thus Mencius too has said.

Kore wa omoi to karui to wakaranū no ja. "Dai wo
heavy light not to distinguish (mono) (de aru) great
This is not to distinguish the weighty from the trifling. It is what

"**sūte-|te, shō wo toru" to mōsu mono de gozarimasū. Nin-jō**
rejecting little to take to call man nature
we call "rejecting the important, and embracing bagatelles." Man's na-

wa ip-|pan shō wa kirai, dai wa suki; karui wa kirai, omoi
as a whole to dislike to like
ture upon the whole is to dislike the small (and) like the great; to dislike the trifling and

wa | suki ja.
to like the important.

Soko de, shinrui yenja ye manekarete, go-chisō ni |
relations connections being invited feast
Now, being invited to relations and connections, at the time

(Notes to page 7.)

Hadzukashii to mo [1], lit., even that (it is) shameful.
Dō iu tokoro, etc., [2], *i.e.*, what can have been the origin of this error.
Yara [3], an interrogative which has not quite the force of demanding an answer, but is rather rhetorical.
Yubi hito, etc. [4], see the rendering and notes, p. 1.
Oserareta [5, 6], an honorific verb, used only of a sage or some exalted personage: 'has deigned to say.'

to onaji koto ja.
same thing (de aru)

Sono danna dono no kokoro ga wadsurai-kurushi-| nde iru
That master Mr. heart being ill and in pain to be
Neglecting the pain and illness of that heart which is the master,

wo sŭtete-oite, kerai no karada bakari | kawaigari, "Hiza-gashira
neglecting servant body only to tend affectionately knee-cap
we nurse the body which is the servant only, "(My) knee is

"suri-muita": "Hokuchi wo tsŭkei"; | "Kiu ga ibōta": "Kōyakŭ
abraded moxa put on blister suppurated plaster
abraded": "Put on a moxa"; "The moxa has suppurated": "Spread

"hare"; "Kaze hiita": "Kakkontō, | nebuka, sōsŭi, shōgazake"
spread garlic hotch-potch ginger-sake
a plaster"; "(I) have caught cold": "An infusion of kakkon, garlic, hotch-potch, ginger-

to; karisome ni mo, karada | no go sewa wa nasare-
thus trifle even trouble altho'
sake," thus (prescribing); altho' one takes trouble for the body even in trifles,

masuredo, kokoro no koto wa ittai | o kamai nashi ja.
one does affair altogether to care is not (de aru)
as to matters which affect the heart one is altogether careless.

Hĭto ni ŭmarete, hĭto no yōna | kokoro mo motazu; oni no
being born sort not to possess devil
Being born a human being, (but) not possessing even a human sort of heart; some-

yōna kokoro wo mottari, kitsŭne no | yōna kokoro wo mottari,
to have sometimes fox
times having a devil's sort of heart, sometimes having a fox's sort of heart,

hebi no yōna kokoro wo mottari, |
snake
sometimes having a snake's sort of heart,

(Notes to page 6.)

Sono, etc. [1], more *lit.*, neglecting the being ill and in pain of that heart which is, etc. When two nouns are in apposition, as *danna* and *kokoro* are here, the Japanese idiom introduces *no* between them. The same remark applies to *kerai* and *karada*, line 2.

Kaze hiita [3], An idiom; *lit.*, have drawn wind.

To [5] *Iute*, saying, or some equivalent verb, *e.g.*, prescribing, must be understood.

Kitsŭne, etc. [8], an allusion to the well-known superstitions of the Japanese concerning foxes.

と頭じ手じや。其日ぐらしの人が。頭ひたし
んぐわるを捨て置く。家来のかしぎぞかり
可哀がり。膝かしつすりむいて。あくちを付けい。
灸がつがよさ。草薬を塗。風ひいて葛根湯
根ぶか雑炊。生姜ざけと。かりそめにも腕伸
の出世となるれしますまいぞ。心の中は一切
體かまひなしじや。人ようすれく人のやうな
こころもをらず。鬼のやうな心を持つ。狐の
やうな心をもつたり。蛇のやうな心を持つ。

ないといやがろうと真似(まね)ります。ソコデ指(ゆび)の人(ひと)に
しかざるが[illegible]なりと申してござりまする。なれど
能(よ)う人も恥(はぢ)を知(し)つてをるのじや。其(その)恥(はぢ)でご
ざりますれ。羞悪(ジウオ)之(ノ)心(ココロハ)義(ギ)之(ノ)端(ハシ)と申して。恥(はぢ)を志る
が人の生(うま)れつき。志りながら其(その)恥(はぢ)を志るふ
二指(あさゆび)でござりまして。姿(すがた)の恥(はぢ)を知(し)りて。心(こころ)の
恥(はぢ)を志らぬ人がござりまする。是(これ)は[illegible](ごまう)
遠(えん)ちがひじや。心(こころ)が大切(たいせつ)なものでござりませ
ね。心(こころ)は[illegible](ぞ)の主(あるじ)とやて。[illegible](らうけん)の内(うち)では[illegible](そんな)どの

nai wo iyagaru kara mairimasŭ. Soko de, "yubi no hĭto ni |
not to be to dislike because to go Therefore finger men
the ordinary run of men's he goes. Therefore it is said, "it is because it (his

"shikazaru ga tame nari" to mōshĭte gozarimasŭ.
to be unlike because to be being said to be
finger) is unlike men's fingers."

Naruhodo | yō hĭto wa haji wo shĭtta mono ja. Sono hadzu
well shame known (de aru) that necessity
Verily, man is a thing knowing shame. It is that ne-

de go-|zarimasŭ. "Shu-wo no kokoro wa gi no hashi" to
shame heart righteousness beginning
cessity. The saying "a heart of shame is the beginning of righteous-

mōshĭte, haji wo shiru | ga hĭto no ŭmare-tsŭki. Shĭkashi nagara,
being said shame to know nature nevertheless
ness" (implies) it is men's nature to know shame. Nevertheless,

sono haji wo shiru ni | fŭta yō gozarimashĭte, sugata no haji wo
two kinds being appearance
in that knowledge of shame there being two kinds, there are men knowing

shĭtte, kokoro no | haji wo shiranŭ hĭto ga gozarimasŭ. Kore wa
knowing not to know this
the shame of appearance who do not know the shame of the heart. This is a

kitsui go riyō-|ken-chigai ja.
violent mistake (de aru)
terrible mistake.

Kokoro hodo taisetsŭ na mono wa gozarimase-|nŭ. "Kokoro
important (naru)
There is no more important thing than the heart. The say-

wa mi no aruji" to mōshĭte, ikken no uchi de wa danna dono |
body master one house master Mr.
ing that "the heart is the lord of the body," is the same thing as the master is one household

---

(Notes to page 5.)

Nai [1], the rest of the verb, must here be taken as a noun: 'the not being.'
Sono hadzu, etc. [3], *i.e.*, nor can it be otherwise.
Shu-wo no kokoro [4], *i.e.*, a sense of shame.
Shiru ni [5], In the knowledge. *Shiri* (root) *ni*, in order to know.
Hĭto [7] is qualified by *shĭtte* and *shiranŭ*.
Hodo [8], *lit.*, amount, quantity; has quite an idiomatic signification here.
"Is the same thing as—" [9], *i.e.*, 'means that—'
Ikken [9], for *ichi-ken; ken* being the numeral for house.

-k'aranū yubi nareba, magatte atte mo, itami saye nakūba | sūtete-
since it is / bent / being / even / pain / only / letting
of which causes no pain, although it ought to make no matter even if let alone

oite yoi hadsu naredomo; moshi kore wo yoku | nobashīte-kureru
alone / good / necessity / although it were / if / this / well
when bent, if there be only no pain; if one should hear that there is a doctor who would

isha dono ga aru to kiitara, michi no | tōi mo itowasu sadamete
doctor / Mr. / is / if should hear / road / distant / even / not caring / certainly
be so kind as to straighten it well, disregarding even a long journey, one would cer-

ryōji wo uke ni yuku de | arō.
treatment / to receive / going / would be
tainly be going to receive treatment.

Sore wa nani yuye? Yubi ga seken no hīto to sūkoshi |
that / what / because / finger / the world / men / a little
And why is this? Because of (your) finger differing slightly from

chigōte aru yuye, hadsukashū oboyete, ryōji wo | ukemasuru no ja.
differing / ashamed / feeling / a receiving / (mono) there is
the generality of men, feeling ashamed, there is a receiving of treatment.

"Shin So no michi" to wa, Shin no kuni to | So no kuni
country
As to the road from Shin to So (*vide* text), the country of Shin in respect to the

to wa, michinori ga sen ri. Kore wa, tōi tokoro wo | itowasu
road measurement / 1000 / this / distant / place
country of So, the distance is 1000 *ri*. This is an illustration of not caring for a dis-

to iu tatoye ja. Kore, sono yubi no hītonami ni |
example / this / that / usual type of man
tant place. Because he dislikes his finger which is not as

(Notes to page 4.)

Magatte, etc. [1], More *lit.*, Although, even being bent (if there be only no pain), letting alone would be necessarily good.

Moshi, etc. [2], More *lit.*, If one should hear that there is a this (finger) well-straightening-to-deign Mr. Doctor.

Tōi [4], Observe the adjective put for an abstract noun. *Tōi* here means distance.

Seken no hīto [5], The men of the world; men in general.

Shin and **So** [7] The ancient names of two provinces in China.

Ri [8], The Chinese *ri* is shorter than the Japanese. The value of the latter is given as 4,275 yards, or about two English miles and two-fifths.

To in line 3 is almost the exact equivalent of 'that.' In line 5 it marks the comparison, and is translated 'from'; so do the second *to* in line 7 and that in line 8. The first *to* in line 7 is the sign of quotation.

Tōi tokoro wo itowasu [8], Disregards a distant place. Does not mind a long journey.

かゝぬ指(ゆび)なれど。ゆがみて有(あつ)ても。いたみさへなくは
捨(すて)ておいても能(よ)い筈(はず)なれども。めつたに気にしてよく
信(のぞ)しくなる医者(いしや)どのがあると聞(きい)たら。町(まち)の
遠(とほ)いもいとはず。さつそく療治(りやうぢ)をうけにゆくで
なからう。それは何故(なぜ)なれば。指(ゆび)が世間(せけん)の人(ひと)と少(すこ)し
違(ちが)ふてゐるゆゑ。恥(はづ)かしうおぼしくて療治(りやうぢ)を
うけまするのじや。晋楚(しんそ)の路(みち)とは。晋(しん)の国(くに)と
楚(そ)の国(くに)とは道法(みちのり)が千里(せんり)。これは遠(とほ)いところを
いとはずといふたものじや。是(これ)其無名(そのむめい)指の人(ひと)なれど

なんが名と為まして。無名指といゝます。何ゆゑ
まく名がないぞといふ。トント用のない指じや。
物を握れば親指小指の力。ほむりとうくれ人
さし指。酒のかんを試るは小指の役。皆それ〴〵
に用がありまする。無名指ばかりは無用の指。
あつく邪魔にならねど。なくて事かけませぬ。
一分のうちでも遊びものじや。其指が風で
のびぬ。勿論つかふこともない。故に疾痛す
不害なうずとしてある。病気なくても苦し

nai ga, na to narimashite, "mŭmei-shi" to mōshimasŭ.
not to be — name — having become — nameless finger — to call
non-existence of a name having become a name, it is called the "nameless finger."

"Nani yuye | mata na ga nai so?" to iu ni; tonto yō no nai
what because — again name — in — at all function
Again, if we ask, 'Why has it no name?'; (the answer is) it is a wholly functionless

yubi ja. | Mono wo nigiru wa oya-yubi ko-yubi no chikara; tsumari
(de aru) things — to grasp — thumb — little finger — strength — head
finger. To take hold of objects is the province of the thumb and little finger; to

wo kaku wa hito- | sashi-yubi; sake no kan wo kokoro-miru wa
to scratch — hot — to test
scratch the head (that of) the first finger; to test hot sake (is) the office of the little finger.

koyubi no yaku. Mina sore-zore | ni yō ga aredomo, mŭmei-shi
office — all — each — although there is
Although there is a function for every one, the nameless finger

bakari wa muyō no yubi, | atte, jama ni narasu; nakŭte, koto wa
only — not-function — being — obstacle — becomes not — not being — things
alone (being) a functionless finger, being (there) it is no obstacle; being absent there

kakemasenŭ. | Isshin no uchi nite mottomo karui mono ja.
not to be imperfect — one body — inside — in — most — unimportant — (de aru)
would be no imperfection. In the whole body it is the most unimportant thing.

Sono yubi ga kagande | nobinu; mochiron itami mo kayumi mo nai.
that — being bent — not to straighten — of course — pain — itching
That finger being bent does not straighten; of course there is neither pain nor itching.

Karu-ga-yuye-ni "shittsŭ koto- | ni gai arasu" to mōshite aru.
wherefore — being said — to be
Wherefore it is said (in the text) that "inflammation causes no particular harm."

Hikkyō nakŭte mo kurushi- |
altogether — even
Since it is a finger even the total absence

(Notes to page 2 continued.)

belongs to all; those which precede being placed in the root form." (Aston's *Written Grammar*, p. 31.) There is a good exemplification of this in the sentence under notice, where the root *ii* occurs thrice before the conclusive form *mōshimasŭ*. In the nomenclature of the fingers both the Japanese and the Chinese names are given and contrasted in each case. **Mōshimasure-do** [8]. It is often convenient, as here, to translate active forms as if they were passive, but the real explanation is that some such word as *hito*, people, (the French *on* and our own 'they') must be understood as a nominative to the verb mōsŭ. **Koto de** (9), *atte*, being, is understood after *de*.

(Notes to page 3.)

Mŭmei shi. It is also called *na nashi yubi*, (*Shingaku Do-wa*, I., p. 5). **Ga** [1] following a verb often shows that the verb is to be taken as a verbal noun, so that *nai* here means 'the not being' or 'the not having.' **To iu ni** [2] more lit., 'in saying that—.' **Sore-zore** [4] The kana has *sore* with the sign of repetition, but the repeated word in such a case takes the nigori. **Sono yubi ga,** etc., [7] This sentence is hypothetical. Supply 'if' or 'supposing that.' See p. 1. **Nobinu** [8] negative of *nobiru*, to stretch, (2nd. conj.) In the sentence, 'India rubber stretches,' the verb would be *nobiru;* in, 'I stretch India rubber,' the verb would be *nobasŭ*. **Itami mo,** etc., [8] Both pain and itching are not. That is, should the third finger become permanently bent, no further disagreeable symptoms occur. It is not an uncommon deformity in this country. **Shittsŭ,** etc., [8] *i.e.*, there is no particular pain or itching to do any harm. **Mōshite** [9] an active form, although translated passively. **Hikkyō,** etc., [9] The literal translation only shows more clearly the "bull" of the original. That figure of speech flourishes in many languages. The anatomy need not be qualified.

-toye wo hiite, hito no kokoro no tai-setsŭ naru koto wo o shime-
-lustration drawing man heart important thing to point
for the heart from which one has diverged," by further deigning to point out by means of

shi | nasareta no de gozarimasŭ. "Ima" to wa, ima koko ni
out (mono) to be here
an illustration the importance of the heart of man. "Now" (in the text) is the word called

to | mōsu koto ja. "Mumei no yubi" to wa, koyubi no tonari
to call thing (de aru) nameless finger little finger neighbour
now here . The "nameless finger" (of the text) is the neighbouring finger

no | yubi de gozarimasŭ. Sono hoka no yubi wa, oya-yubi wo
of those other as to parent
to the little finger . As to the other fingers , the thumb is called

dai- | shi to ii; hito-sashi-yubi wo tō-shi to ii; taka-daka-yubi | wo
great finger to say to point head high high
the great finger; the index-finger is called the head finger; the tallest finger is called the

chu-shi to ii; ko-yubi wo shō-shi to mōshimasŭ. Tada, | koyubi
middle little to call only
middle finger; the little finger is called the little finger. Only there is not a

no tonari no yubi ni na ga nai. Mottomo, beni - sashi - yubi |
name not to be certainly vermillion to stick
name for the neighbouring finger to the little finger. Although it is quite true that it is

to wa mōshimasŭredo, kore wa go fujin gata bakari no | koto de
although called this woman (plural) only term
called the rouge-putting-finger, this being only a woman's term

tenka tsūyō de wa gozarimasenŭ. Soko de, na no |
whole nation current not to be therewithal name
is not current throughout the kingdom. Therewithal, the

(Notes to page 1 continued.)

in the text must be taken in the sense of the general run of men. 'Ordinary men's fingers' in the translation gives the sense. **Yubi no hito ni shikazaru.** The *no* goes with *shikazaru* and not with *hito*. **Tagui,** etc. The meaning is that crookedness of one's finger and crookedness of heart belong to the same class, and one ought to be equally ashamed of both. **Sate,** etc. [6] Here begins the preacher's discourse. **Benjimashita** [7] must be taken as an adjective qualifying the phrase which follows, down to *shō*. In English a relative clause would be introduced, such as "which I explained last night." **De** [8] marks the predicate of the proposition. **Hō-shin.** This expression indicates a theory the very reverse of that of Original Sin. In the philosophy of Mencius man is born with an originally pure nature (*hon-shin*) to revert to which is the object of all virtuous aspirations. **To iu koto ni yotte,** referring to the statement that, etc.

(Notes to page 2.)

Shimeshi nasareta no [1, 2] lit., a having-deigned-to-point-out thing. **"Ima,"** etc., [2] The preacher clears the way by giving the audience a necessary explanation of his Chinese text. **Wa** [2] There is considerable confusion in the statements of grammarians as to this particle. It is often found with the nominative case, but its full force is selective and contrasting, and frequently can best be translated by *as to*. "*Wa* is a distinctive or separative particle. It has the force of isolating or singling out one object from among a number, or of opposing one thing to another. In English the same idea is usually expressed not by a separate word but by means of a greater emphasis on the noun. *Wa* has frequently very little meaning, and its presence or absence is often immaterial." (Aston's *Spoken Grammar*, 3rd. ed., p. 3.) **To mōsŭ** [2, 3] is called, *i.e.*, means. **De** [2 and 4] the mark of the predicate. Line 2. **Kono shō,** 'this verse,' which may be supplied after *sunawachi*, is the nominative to *gozarimasŭ*. **Ii** [5 and 6], root of *iu*, to say or call. Note the important rule of Japanese syntax, that "when two or more verbs are co-ordinated in the same sentence, the last only receives the inflection which properly [belongs

とへと引ば。人の心は大切なる事を御志し
なされるのでござりまして。今もって
申す事じや。無名の指とは小指の隣の
指でござります。其中の指は親ゆびを大
指といひ。人さしゆびを頭指といひ。高き指
を中指といひ。小指を小指と申ます。なぐ
小指の隣のゆびは名が無い。むべさし指
とは申ますれども。是を御婦人がたは紅の
るすぐ。天下通用でハござりませぬ。ソコデ名の

鳩翁道話弐之上

男　武修聞書

孟子曰。今有無名之指屈而不信非疾痛害事也。如有能信之者則不遠晋楚之路為指之不若人也。指不若人則知悪之。心不若人則不知悪。此之謂不知類也。さて
これまで段々弁じました。仁人心也の次乃章でござります。則學問之道無他求其放心而已矣といふ言ふなく。孟子ましく。た

KIU-Ō DŌ-WA.

Kiu-O's Sermons on Moral Subjects.

Ni no jō.
Two of upper.
First (part) of the second (volume).

Dan Bu-shu bun sho.
Son to hear to write.
Bu-shu, son (of the preacher) took it down.

Mōshi no iwaku, "Ima mūmei no yubi ari, kagande
Mencius to say now nameless finger to be being bent
A saying of Mencius: "Now there is the nameless finger, having become deformed,

"**nobisu. Shittsū koto-ni gai aru ni arasu. Moshi yoku kore**
flexes not itching & pain particularly harm to be not to be If well this
it flexes not. The itching and pain are not particularly harmful. If there be a man who

"**wo noburu mono aru toki wa, sunawachi Shin So no michi tōshi**
to straighten person to be time then (conj.) way distant
can well straighten it , then the way from Shin to So he makes not

"**to sesū, yubi no hito ni shikazaru ga tame nari; yubi**
not to make men to be unlike because to be
too far , because it is unlike ordinary men's fingers ; when

"**hito ni shikazaru toki wa, sunawachi kore wo nikumu koto wo**
to time this to dislike affair
the finger is unlike ordinary men's fingers, then he feels this a thing he dislikes

"**shiru; kokoro hito ni shikazaru toki wa, sunawachi nikumu koto**
to feel heart
; when the heart is unlike ordinary men's hearts, then he does not feel that

"**wo shirasu. Kore wo tagui wo shiranū to iu." Sate, | kore wa**
not to feel class not to know to say now
it is any dislike. This is called ignorance of classes. Now, this is the verse

semban benjimashita, "Jin wa hito no kokoro nari" no tsugi no |
previous evening explained benevolence man heart to be next
which follows the (verse I) explained last evening, (viz:—) "Benevolence is the heart of man

shō de gozarimasū. Sunawachi, "Gakū-mon no michi ta nashi sono
verse to be namely learning path other is not that
That is to say, it is a text in which Mencius follows up the

"**hō-shin wo motomuru nomi," to iu koto ni yotte, Mōshi mata ta- |**
diverged heart to seek alone to referring further il-
statement that "the path of learning is nothing more than the seeking

---

Kiu-O [1] The name of the preacher. **Dō-wa** [1] Way-discourse. The phrase *michi no hanashi* is substituted in the *Shingaku* sermons. The meaning is 'discourse on the Path,' *i.e.*, the path of virtue, the "narrow way" in fact. **Jō** [1] upper, *i.e.*, first of two parts. **Ima**, etc. [3] Here begins the preacher's text, which is all written in Chinese, with square characters. Where these are employed throughout the sermon the sentences are pure Chinese. The marks which indicate the transposition of the words, and the Japanese *katakana* rendering at the side (called *wa-kun*) are but rude glosses for the uneducated. The construction and grammar of the *wakun* are often barely tolerable, and the words and phrases differ much from the spoken dialect, in which this sermon is written; *e.g.*, *ta nashi* in the second quotation on this page would probably be *hoka wa nai* in the spoken dialect. The greater portion of the text is amplified and explained in the course of the sermon. "It may be well to warn the student against the interlinear translations which often accompany Japanese editions of Chinese books. It is sufficient to say that as regards grammar and style they are barely on a par with the worst of the interlinear translations of Latin and Greek works which are sometimes seen in the hands of schoolboys in this country." (Aston's *Written Grammar*, p. iv.)

Division of Lines.—Where Chinese occurs it is sometimes impossible to show the divisions, because of the inversions of the characters necessary to produce even an indifferent Japanese.

Iwaku [3] a verbal noun formed by adding *ku* to the negative base of the verb. This form is foreign to the spoken language, and is not common even in the written language. **Kagande** [3] the deformity being hypothetical we must supply 'if' or 'supposing that' before *kagande*. **Toki**, lit. 'time'; also 'when' or 'if.' **Tōshi** would be **tōi** in the spoken language. **Hito**

[in

www.ingramcontent.com/pod-product-compliance
Lightning Source LLC
Chambersburg PA
CBHW021946160426
43195CB00011B/1233